Looking Out
for #1

Looking Out for #1

How to Get from

Where You Are Now to

Where You Want to Be in Life

ROBERT RINGER

Skyhorse Publishing

Copyright © 2013 by Robert Ringer

All Rights Reserved. No part of this book may be reproduced in any manner without the express written consent of the publisher, except in the case of brief excerpts in critical reviews or articles. All inquiries should be addressed to Skyhorse Publishing, 307 West 36th Street, 11th Floor, New York, NY 10018.

Skyhorse Publishing books may be purchased in bulk at special discounts for sales promotion, corporate gifts, fund-raising, or educational purposes. Special editions can also be created to specifications. For details, contact the Special Sales Department, Skyhorse Publishing, 307 West 36th Street, 11th Floor, New York, NY 10018 or info@skyhorsepublishing.com.

Skyhorse® and Skyhorse Publishing® are registered trademarks of Skyhorse Publishing, Inc.®, a Delaware corporation.

www.skyhorsepublishing.com

10 9 8 7 6 5 4 3 2 1

Library of Congress Cataloging-in-Publication Data is available on file.

ISBN: 978-1-62636-040-2

Printed in the United States of America

Dedicated to the hope that somewhere in our universe there exists a civilization whose inhabitants possess sole dominion over their own lives, where every individual has the ability to recognize and the courage to acknowledge reality, and where governments as we know them do not exist.

Contents

Introduction

Given that the term *looking out for number one* has been so distorted by an army of media people who never took the trouble to read the book, I would like to clearly define it at the outset: Looking out for number one is the conscious effort to make rational decisions that lead to the greatest amount of happiness over the long term, so long as the actions stemming from those decisions do not involve the use of force or fraud against anyone else. In simpler terms, looking out for number one begins with the belief that you have a moral right to take actions aimed at giving you the greatest amount of pleasure and least amount of pain, provided your actions do not violate the rights of others.

It goes without saying that someone else's ego being harmed by your happiness or success, or his[1*] experiencing deep emotional pain as a result of his uncontrolled envy of you, does not equate to aggression. Such an unfortunate mind-set stems from the

---

[1*] Because I find it cumbersome to use hybrid pronouns such as "his/hers" and am opposed to debasing the English language by mixing singular nouns and pronouns with plural pronouns such as "they," I have, for the sake of convenience only, chosen to use the masculine gender throughout this book in most instances where the neuter has not been employed.

afflicted person's own neuroses, and by no stretch of the imagination is it your job to spend your waking hours trying to heal sick minds—unless, of course, you're a psychologist, in which case I would suggest you would be a lot more productive if you would have the neurotic individual in question call your receptionist for an appointment.

It's also important to understand that the idea of looking out for number one is neither narcissistic nor hedonistic, because focusing on personal happiness does not preclude your being kind, charitable, or civic-minded. Nor does it prevent you from being a team player or building meaningful, enduring relationships. On the contrary, all these, and more, can result in long-term happiness for you.

An important tenet of looking out for number one, however, is that you have no moral obligation to submit to playing the role of sacrificial lamb whose interests, goals, and happiness are always subordinated to the interests, goals, and happiness of everyone with whom you come in contact—particularly those whom you do not count among your friends or loved ones. Trying to please everyone is a well-known formula for unhappiness.

Clearly, then, not only does your achieving happiness and success not in any way harm others, it also puts you in a position to make constructive contributions to those closest to you and, through the invisible hand of the marketplace, even people you will never even meet.

1 Looking Out for Number One

As stated in the Introduction, whenever I use the term *looking out for number one* I am referring to the conscious effort to make rational decisions that lead to the greatest amount of happiness over the long term, so long as the actions stemming from those decisions do not involve the use of force or fraud against anyone else.

Long-term thinking is a critical aspect of looking out for number one, because short-term pleasure can be self-destructive if not weighed against long-term consequences. If, for example, one engages in armed robbery, the fruits of his crime may bring him short-term pleasure. However, the long-term result—hiding and/ or incarceration—is sure to bring pain that will far outweigh his short-term gains. It is self-evident that thinking only short term is not a rational way to live one's life. I bow to Ayn Rand on the subject:

> A rational man . . . does not live his life short-range and does not drift like a bum pushed by the spur of the moment. It means that he does not regard any moment as cut off from the context of the rest of his life, and that he allows no conflicts or contradictions between his short-range and long-range interests. He does not become his own destroyer by pursuing a desire today which wipes out all his values tomorrow.

Knowingly or unknowingly, everyone tries to make decisions that lead to more pleasure and less pain, but such decisions are not always rational. To make rational decisions, you have to be aware of *what* you're doing and *why* you're doing it. If you wish to consciously and consistently make wise pleasure/pain decisions, it is necessary to lift your consciousness to a high level of awareness. This means elevating your thought processes to a point that gives you the capacity to act out of choice—*your* choice—a majority of the time.

While the high point on your mental awareness meter is taking action based only on your own rational choices, the low point is taking action based on what others choose for you. If you're in the habit of not basing your actions on rational choice, you're out of control, and anyone out of control is dangerous both to himself and those around him. In the event this describes your way of life, today is the best day to begin taking steps toward curing this self-destructive habit.

Looking out for number one is a transforming philosophy that can bring about dramatic changes in your life. When practiced honestly and consistently, it will give you the power to replace financial pressure with financial stability. It will result in warm, meaningful relationships in place of never-ending conflicts with people who bring mostly pain into your life. It will give you more free time in place of a harried life in which you never seem to have

enough time for anything. It will give you a clear mind in place of a mind cluttered and stressed.

On a broader scale, looking out for number one will lead you to the realization that life is worth living and that it can and should be a pleasant, meaningful, exciting experience. The natural offspring of this discovery are feelings of self-control and self-esteem, which in turn perpetuate a positive state of mind and an action-oriented life.

Consciously or unconsciously, everyone's main objective in life is to be as happy as possible. But what, exactly, is happiness? Wise men have been arguing over the definition of this elusive term since the beginning of recorded history. I choose to define happiness in simple terms: *one's state of mind when he is experiencing pleasure.*

If happiness is the main objective, then all other objectives are really only a means to accomplishing happiness. Therefore, to the degree our subobjectives are rational, and to the degree we achieve them, we tend to experience what we refer to as *happiness.*

It's also important to recognize that there is no such thing as absolute happiness. Happiness comes in degrees. You can be happier today than yesterday, twice as happy yesterday as you were the day before, and hope to be much happier tomorrow than you are today. The degree of your happiness at any given moment will depend upon the rationality of your decisions and actions, as well as the success you have in achieving your subobjectives. The more rational your decisions and actions, the more often you will experience results that lead to happiness.

YOUR WEIGHT-AND-BALANCE HAPPINESS SCALE

Your cerebral computer, commonly referred to as the *brain,* contains a biological computer chip I like to think of as your *Weight-and-Balance Happiness Scale.* This remarkable scale automatically weighs every known alternative available to you at any given time and chooses the one it believes will result in the greatest amount of happiness for you. The only problem with your Weight-and-Balance Happiness Scale is that it sometimes malfunctions; i.e., it doesn't always ascertain the facts correctly and therefore does not always produce decisions that are in your long-term best interest.

So, as with any computer, it's only as good as the operator who feeds it information. If you feed your Weight-and-Balance Happiness Scale irrational thoughts, it will make irrational decisions. That's why there is no escaping the reality that it's up to you to keep your scale functioning properly. It will never fail to make a decision for you, and each decision will be what it believes to be in your best interest at any particular point in time. Even the failure to make a decision is, in fact, a decision—the decision *not* to take action. The batting average of your Weight-and-Balance Happiness Scale is directly related to your level of awareness and your determination to take only rational actions.

But there's another factor that comes into play with your Weight-and-Balance Happiness Scale. Even if we all exercised good reasoning powers before taking action, each of us would seek happiness in our own way. Some pursue happiness by becoming martyrs, others by being well read and knowledgeable on a variety of subjects, and still others by accumulating great wealth.

The differences in our pursuits are due to our varying ideas about what happiness is, i.e., what leads to our experiencing the greatest amount of pleasure. Of and by itself, this divergence of views is not a bad thing. It's only when others try to tell you what should make you happy that problems begin to appear. And when that occurs, you do yourself a great disservice if you believe that the opinions of others should be binding on you.

How can you be certain that your Weight-and-Balance Happiness Scale is functioning properly? The pleasure/pain compartments of your brain will always give you an easy-to-read printout; i.e., you will either feel happy or unhappy. The happier you are, the more your scale is in balance; the unhappier you are, the more your scale is telling you that something about your thoughts and actions are out of sync. The greater the happiness you hope to achieve, the greater the price you should expect to pay. It is, of course, up to you to decide the price you're willing to pay, but it's wise to decide on that price *before* taking action.

Aside from paying the price necessary for a better life, your only other option is inaction, i.e., accepting things as they are and living with the frustration, conflict, and pain that make life more of a burden than a celebration. Unfortunately, most people choose inaction, because inaction is the easiest alternative. In effect, the choice they make through their inaction is to avoid relatively mild, short-term pain in exchange for a lifetime of dull, chronic pain— and dull, chronic pain is a virtual living death. Why worry about life after death if you're not living this one?

The wisest, long-term choice is to commit to the effort—no matter how difficult it may be—to take positive, rational action every day of your life. This may mean making radical changes in your lifestyle, occupation, or place of residence. Such changes, of course, should be made only after careful reasoning convinces you they are warranted, because much of what it takes to make you happy may be right under your nose. Or, as an unknown author once put it, the bird in the hand looks awfully good after it's already left your hand.

WINNING

Is winning necessary to happiness? Since happiness is a result of accomplishing a series of subobjectives, winning in areas that are most important to you is bound to make you happier than losing. However, if a person's subobjectives are a result of bad choices, or if he has too many important subobjectives, the result can be frustration and disappointment.

While the problem of choosing inappropriate subobjectives usually stems from irrational thinking, having too many subobjectives is often a result of buying into the generally accepted notion that winning at everything is admirable. When people say, "He's a winner," what they usually mean is that a person is an overachiever. "He's competitive" conjures up images of a tense individual who never takes time to relax, who tends to go all out whether he's negotiating a business deal or playing a weekend game of golf.

However, when I think of winning, I don't necessarily equate it to the highest score. For example, your objectives when playing tennis on a Saturday afternoon might be to relax and enjoy the company of another person. If at the end of your match you're relaxed and feel as though you've had a good time, then you've "won." Unless it's competitive tennis, whether or not you end up with the winning score should not be the critical issue. Winning merely for the sake of winning elevates it to an end in itself, and thereby relegates the main objective—happiness—to a position of lesser importance. That's often the predicament of the person who's main focus is on making money. He gets so caught up in accumulating wealth that he forgets to take the time to enjoy it.

That's why it's wise to put a lot of thought into deciding which subobjectives are most important to your happiness, then set your priorities accordingly. Don't place an equal value on becoming a great tennis player, a renowned socialite, a successful businessperson, a gourmet cook, and a top-flight poker player—unless your idea of happiness is exhaustion, stress, and high blood pressure.

An obsessively competitive attitude can lead to several bad consequences. It can drain you of energy that is needed to accomplish more important objectives. It can make you look foolish for trying to compete fiercely in an activity into which you are not willing or able to put the necessary time and effort or for which you do not possess much natural ability. It can cause enormous frustration, which in turn can adversely affect your attitude when it comes to facing more important challenges. Finally, an obsessively competitive attitude can cause strained relationships with people who might otherwise be valuable allies.

The reality is that, regardless of how hard you try, you can't have all the candy in the store, if for no other reason than because neither you nor anyone else possesses enough time, energy, or talent to gain such a monopoly. This being the case, why frustrate your-self trying to win at everything? Leave some for the rest of us, because we're going to get our share whether you like it or not. That's because, collectively, we possess greater talent than you in many areas, or it may simply be because we're able to devote more time and energy than you to one area or another. Time is a fixed commodity that limits what you can accomplish during your life-time. Thus, rather than helping you achieve happiness, the obses-sion to win at everything may only succeed in driving you mad.

IS IT MORAL?

Is looking out for number one moral? As a preface to answering this all-important question, I should first describe the Absolute Moralist, a nemesis of all people of goodwill. The lifetime mission of the Absolute Moralist is to badger you into doing the "right thing"—as defined by him, of course. Like Satan, the Absolute Moralist disguises himself in a variety of human forms. He may make his appearance as a politician, an environmentalist, or even your next-door neighbor.

Whatever his disguise, however, you can count on the Absolute Moralist to be relentless. He is the self-appointed guardian of the law. He's the guy who shakes his fist and honks his horn at you for a full block because you inadvertently moved into his lane without what he considered to be proper clearance. It is his moral duty to make certain you understand that you've committed a heinous crime.

The Absolute Moralist will stalk you to your grave if you allow him to do so. If he senses you're a ripe target—that you do not base your actions on rational self-choice—he will punish you unmerci-fully, making guilt your bedfellow until he convinces you that you are a subpar human being.

Above all, the Absolute Moralist is a humanlike creature whose main focus in life is to decide what's right for you. If he gives to a certain charity, he will try to shame you into understanding that it's your moral duty to give to the same charity. If he believes in a religious doctrine, he is certain that it's his moral duty to help you "see the light." In the most extreme cases, he may even feel morally obliged to kill you in order to save you from your disbelief.

In summation, the main objective of an Absolute Moralist is to control your life. He does not understand that appealing to *your* needs is the best way to motivate you to add value to *his* life. The simplest way to get the Absolute Moralist to leave you alone is to make the firm decision not to allow him to impose his beliefs on you, because it is totally within your power to do so.

I would suggest that in deciding whether or not it is moral to look out for number one, the first thing you should do is eliminate from consideration the unsolicited opinions of others. Morality—the quality of right and wrong—is a very personal and private matter, thus no one possesses the right to decide what is right or wrong for you. So long as your idea of right and wrong does not include committing aggression against others, and so long as it falls reasonably within the generally accepted code of conduct of the society in which you live, you have a right to pursue your happiness in anyway you so choose.

I suggest that you make a prompt and thorough effort to eliminate from your life all people who claim—either through their words or actions—to possess the right to force you to abide by their notion of right and wrong.

What It Does Not Mean

While looking out for number one involves making decisions that result in more pleasure and less pain, it does not give you carte blanche to commit aggression against others. In addition to the obvious immorality of aggression, there is a rational reason why forcible interference in the lives of others has no place in the philosophy of looking out for number one: It simply is not in your best interest. In the long run, sticking your nose in other people's business will bring you more pain than pleasure, which is the opposite of what looking out for number one is all about.

It is, of course, possible for someone to experience short-term pleasure by violating the rights of others, but the long-term losses from such actions are almost certain to more than offset the short-term pleasure experienced. Why? Because the bad-cause/bad-effect syndrome is a cosmic reality. Actions always beget appropriate consequences. A person must either abide by this universal law or be prepared to suffer the consequences.

WHY NOT?

Perhaps the question "Is it moral to look out for number one?" can best be answered with another question: Can you think of any rational reason why you should *not* try to make your life more pleasurable and less painful, so long as your actions do not harm anyone else? You have but one life to live. Is there anything unreasonable about nurturing that life and doing everything within your power to make it pleasant and fulfilling? Is there anything wrong with being aware of what you're doing and why you're doing it? Is it unreasonable to act out of free choice rather than the choice of others?

It's noble to give top priority to the needs of loved ones, because their happiness is often the greatest source of your happiness. But raw, indiscriminate self-sacrifice is another matter altogether. Actions based on the latter are usually committed under the influence of a low awareness level. The truth is that, in the long run, such artificial altruism is likely to make you resentful over what you've forfeited as a result of your actions. While your intentions may be above reproach, it's a grave mistake to repeatedly and indiscriminately sacrifice your own well-being to the needs of everyone who happens to stumble into your life—or, worse, people who aren't even in your life.

The sad irony is that if you persist in swimming in the dangerous and uncivilized waters of self-sacrifice, those for whom you supposedly sacrifice will often be worse off for your efforts. If, instead, you focus your efforts on looking out for number one, those people you care about most will actually benefit from your actions, because it will put you in a position to be far more helpful to them. It's only when you try to pervert the laws of nature and make everyone else's happiness your first responsibility that you run into trouble. The idea that self-sacrifice is virtuous is, in fact, a fiction created by those who aspire to control the lives of others. (Think politicians.)

That looking out for number one brings happiness to others, in addition to being in your own best interest, is one of the great poetic justices of life. At best, looking out for number one benefits you and others; at worst, it benefits only you, but does no harm to anyone else. However, even in the latter case, looking out for number one is actually a benefit to others, because when you're content and happy, you aren't a potential burden to the rest of society.

Which, in my opinion, is more than enough reason to view looking out for number one as a noble pursuit. As a bonus, when you practice the principles of looking out for number one you will find it easier to develop rewarding relationships, because happy people tend to be much more gracious, kind, compassionate, and charitable than those who are unhappy.

IS IT EASY?

If you're a mature adult, you already know that to accomplish anything worthwhile takes effort. Nevertheless, millions of people seem incapable of grasping this self-evident truth. Virtually everyone is familiar with Murphy's Law, but it's worth repeating.

> *Nothing is as easy as it looks,*
> *Everything takes longer than you expect,*
> *And if anything can go wrong, it will,*
> *At the worst possible moment.*

One of the reasons Murphy's Law is timeless is the reality that nothing seems to stay in one place long enough to pin it down. Like a greased watermelon, just when you think you have it under control, it manages to slip from your grasp. This phenomenon is underscored by the **Changing-Circumstances Theory**, which states: *The one thing in life you can absolutely count on is that circumstances will continually change. The great unknown is when they will change.*

That being the case, enjoy life, but be flexible in your planning. It's dangerous to base your decisions on the assumption that everything is going to continue as it now is. It won't. Worse, because circumstances have a habit of changing with little warning, you are often caught off guard.

One day you're on top of the world financially; the next day you're staring bankruptcy in the face because of a competitor's new product or a bad economy. Today you look forward to getting to the office; tomorrow you have a new supervisor you dislike. For years you've been accustomed to playing golf twice a week; suddenly, you have a back problem and your doctor says you should forget about golf and take up swimming.

Relatives die, friends move away, buildings are torn down and replaced by new ones. Changing tastes catch a performer by surprise and make him into a has-been; an athlete discovers he doesn't fit in with the new coach's plans and is out of a job; a mid-level executive finds himself unemployed when his company closes down his division. Nothing lasts forever, and the individual who is not attuned to that reality is likely to be unnecessarily vulnerable to inevitable bumps in the road. He is constantly caught off balance and finds himself unprepared to make the rational decisions necessary to leading a happy, fulfilling life.

On the other hand, the better you understand the reality that circumstances constantly change, the more likely you are to make rational decisions. Your best insurance policy in this regard is to be found in the old adage "You can't win 'em all." In fact, a more accurate perspective would be to say that you can't *lose* 'em all. Because lose you will—and often. It's just the way life is.

Losses are built into your life's equation by constant change and factors beyond your control. If you don't understand this reality, you're likely to end up with a shattered self-image and buckets of frustration following each failure. But if you acknowledge the reality that life has an annoying habit of not cooperating with your plans, your brain does not self-destruct whenever an obstacle arises. In addition, you will be far more likely to be prepared to take advantage of it when things finally do fall into place. Thus, even though you accept the reality that life is fraught with adversity, you do more than just hope for the best. You *prepare* for it.

While enduring life's bumps and bruises in a daily stream of lost battles, each time you stumble you should make it a point to extract the lesson learned and use your newfound knowledge to be better prepared the next time around. The bad experience is history, so let go of it. Instead, focus on the knowledge you've gained, because that knowledge can prove to be far more valuable than the fruits of victory. The following anecdote from David Seabury does an excellent job of making this point:

> In South Africa, they dig for diamonds. Tons of earth are moved to find a little pebble not as large as a little fingernail. The miners are looking for the diamonds, not the dirt. They are willing to lift all the dirt in order to find the jewels. In daily life, people forget this principle and become pessimists because there is more dirt than diamonds. When trouble comes, don't be frightened by the negatives. Look for the positives and dig them out. They are so valuable it doesn't matter if you have to handle tons of dirt.

Understanding that adversity and obstacles are an integral part of life will make it far easier for you to move the dirt between you and *your* diamonds. It's all part of the price you pay for success. You are much ahead of the game if you accept the reality that everything in life has a price. That includes love, friendship, financial reward, peace of mind, the freedom to come and go as you please—anything that adds pleasure to your existence. If you delude yourself into believing otherwise, you will repeatedly learn the hard way that actions do indeed have consequences.

This principle is so important to me that I've developed the habit of consciously trying to ascertain, in advance, the price of anything I desire. Whether the required payment be in time, money, energy, discomfort, or any other form of currency, I try not to kid myself about it. And once I've made up my mind that something is worth the price, I like to pay that price as quickly as possible and get it over with. The sooner the payment is out of the way, the sooner you can get on with enjoying what you've acquired.

What I'm talking about here is long-term solutions versus short-term patching. Dispense with the rationalization that you can temporarily resolve a problem just to get past a rough spot in your path, with the intention of working out a more permanent solution at some unspecified future date. Such a date has a habit of never arriving, and, as a result, the problem only festers and grows. You can't buy happiness on an installment plan. Begin paying the price today so you can start enjoying the benefits as soon as possible. And rest assured that no one is going to make the payments for you.

In the coming pages, the ball will be in your court. I wish I could be the bearer of good tidings and tell you that you have unlimited time to stare at the ball and decide what you're going to do with it, but that's not reality. Like all games, the game of life must end—and the clock is ticking as you read this.

How much time? No one knows for certain, but the average life span is roughly eighty years, so it's wise to look at anything beyond that number as a windfall. As an example, the moment you turn twenty-five (and assuming you will live to the age of eighty), you have precisely 20,075 days left on this earth, or about 2,867 weeks. That's 660 months! Choose the lifespan that makes you feel most comfortable when doing your calculations, but never lose sight of the fact that the clock is ticking.

2 The Reality Hurdle

In order to clear the Reality Hurdle you must become a realist. A realist is a person who believes in basing his life on facts and has little interest in anything that seems imaginary, impractical, theoretical, or utopian.

The biggest problem most people have with reality is that they tend to confuse it with their likes and dislikes. One's personal feelings regarding a reality are not relevant to the reality itself; scorning someone ("the messenger") for pointing out a reality does not alter that reality; and to deceive oneself about reality is the worst of all possible worlds—a habit that in extreme cases can be fatal. In the words of Bishop Butler, "Things and actions are what they are, and the consequences of them will be what they will be; why then should we desire to be deceived?"

Proper perception of reality is as crucial to life as oxygen. Trying to make it through life without a solid grasp of reality is like stumbling around in a dark room laden with land mines. Being aware of what you're doing and why you're doing it—a prerequisite for looking out for number one—means being conscious of what's going on around you. An understanding of reality gives you the foundation for making rational choices rather than allowing your actions to be based on impulse or the choice of others.

The **Theory of Reality** states: *Reality is neither the way you wish things to be nor the way they appear to be, but the way they actually are. Either you acknowledge reality and use it to your benefit or it will automatically work against you.*

The fact that reality works against you if you choose to ignore it is what makes life such a tough journey for so many people. Which is good for me, because if life were easy, you probably wouldn't feel the need to read this book. Instead, you could be living the carefree, glamorous life that Madison Avenue depicts for us on television.

But, alas, life is not as Madison Avenue portrays it. Life is not a suave-looking hunk decked out in a tuxedo, lounging on a bearskin rug in front of a fireplace and sipping cognac with a sensuous woman clad in a black satin gown. (Do these people ever work? Or fight for parking spaces? Or spill their cognac?) Neither is life your friendly neighborhood insurance agent appearing at your side, like a genie out of a bottle, whenever a little problem arises—like your house burning down.

The reality is that life is filled with bad stuff. Life is Janis Ian's seventies classic, "At Seventeen":

> To those of us who knew the pain
> Of valentines that never came,
> And those whose names were never called
> When choosing sides for basketball.
> It was long ago, and far away,
> The world was younger than today,
> And dreams were all they gave for free
> To ugly duckling girls like me.

It's good to have a positive attitude about life, but it's also important to recognize that life is fraught with difficulties. The more you accept the reality that life is a never-ending series of adversities and obstacles, the more likely you are to remain positive about achieving long-term results. And the good news is that no one can stop you from taking action to overcome the adversities and obstacles in your path.

The danger of confusing personal desires with reality is explained in the **Is's versus *Ought-to's* Theory**, which states: *The degree of complications in a person's life corresponds to the degree to which he dwells on the way he thinks the world ought to be rather than the way it actually is.*

I think there *ought to* be no such thing as prejudice—racial, religious, or sexual.

I think there *ought to* be a way to eliminate human rights violations in all countries.

In fact, I think the world *ought to* have no governments or nations at all. I think it should consist of billions of free individuals who have the right to do whatever they please, so long as they do not commit aggression against others.

Many even believe that there *ought to* be no necessity to work for a living. Why shouldn't people have everything they want without having to spend most of their waking hours working? It's not hard to understand why clueless college kids become so excited when introduced to Marxism for the first time.

And how about a gorgeous, intelligent, understanding woman for every man, and a handsome, intelligent, understanding man for every woman? Surely everyone would agree that this *ought to* be a reality.

While we're at it, there also *ought to* be no need to waste a third of your life sleeping, there *ought to* be no such thing as death, and there *ought to* be a real Santa Claus.

Isn't it great to fantasize? For a moment there, I got so carried away thinking about all the things that *ought to* be that I almost managed to hypnotize myself. And that's exactly what an ought-to life is—a life of self-hypnosis, a life based on fantasy rather than reality.

It's easy to fall into the trap of allowing your desires and emotions to play tricks on you by creating illusions intended to pass for reality. Unfortunately, while a person spends his time dwelling on *ought to's*—and makes decisions accordingly—the world continues on its merry way dealing in *is's*. Of and by itself, of course, the fact that your wishes are irrelevant to reality would not be so bad. It's only when you start substituting wishes for reality that you become a magnet for disaster.

Is living in an unreal world of *ought to's* really all that bad? I can best answer that by asking another question: Is it really so terrible for a person to jump off a ten-story building because he believes that man ought to be able to fly? This may be a farfetched example, but it graphically illustrates the dangers that lie in the path of the person who lives in a world of *ought to's*. Such an individual may succeed in acting out of choice, but it will not be *rational* choice. You cannot make rational decisions unless you are aware. And if you do not have the ability and courage to recognize and acknowledge reality, you are certain to be unaware.

REALITY VERSUS PERCEPTION OF REALITY

I have often heard it argued that reality is not an absolute, that each individual has his own perception of reality. The implication is that because each of us perceives the world through our own eyes, reality itself changes from person to person. While it's true that everyone perceives reality differently, reality could care less about our perceptions. Reality does not change to adapt to our viewpoints; reality is what *is*. Reality is fact. Reality is truth.

Reality, however, is not always *known*, and that's where *perception* of reality comes in. While reality is a fixed factor in the equation of life, perception of reality is a variable. Which means that you must learn to differentiate between a principle and an opinion. The most significant aspect of a principle is that it can neither be created nor altered. Thus, a principle is the essence of reality. It is what it is, and it's up to us to discover it. The problem arises when people refuse to accept the reality that principles can only be discovered, and instead choose to believe they can create their own principles. Which means they believe they can create their own reality, a belief that can lead to disastrous consequences.

There are an infinite number of natural laws to be discovered, but, fortunately, you don't have to have a detailed understanding of every one of them to achieve your goals. However, there is one law with which you must be totally familiar and which you must unfailingly use as a guide for your actions. The law I am referring to is the ultimate, immutable law of nature, the foundation of reality itself: *Actions have consequences.* Although I believe most of us intellectually understand the inherent truth of this principle, firsthand observation has convinced me that very few people give it more than a passing thought as they go about their daily lives.

Why would people ignore such an all-powerful, immutable principle? Because truth can often be harsh, and, as human beings, we quite naturally gravitate toward less pain and more pleasure. We simply do not like our little self-delusive worlds to be upset by such a trivial matter as truth. We don't worry about consequences we may have to deal with tomorrow; we just want to feel good today. Unfortunately, we only succeed in deluding ourselves when we engage in such shallow thinking. The reality is that one must be willing to experience the discomfort often associated with truth if his objective is to achieve positive, long-term results.

Another major obstacle to an accurate perception of reality is what I like to refer to as the Paradigm Restriction. We are all confined not only to the planet on which we live, but, metaphorically speaking, we reside within our own mental worlds. It is difficult to comprehend ideas and circumstances we are not accustomed to hearing and seeing within the invisible parameters that surround our lives.

In other words, one of the causes of our differing perceptions of truth is that we all start from our own set of assumptions. This is precisely the reason why the serious seeker of truth must learn to question everything and be willing to give up cherished notions, even if it means suffering discomfort. The best antidote for the Paradigm Restriction is an open mind. This requires rejection of custom and tradition as a basis of fact, and, in its place, acceptance of logic and reason. Clearing the Reality Hurdle requires that you learn to correctly perceive reality and have the courage to accept it—which is where the Mr. Magoos and Ostriches encounter most of their problems.

A Mr. Magoo is someone who simply does not have the mental capacity to correctly perceive reality. He's the individual who truly believes, in spite of mountains of evidence to the contrary, that pie-in-the-sky business deals can be closed, that politicians are better equipped than he is to determine what is best for him, and that other people will act in his best interest and subordinate their own interests to his needs. Which means, in simple terms, that a Mr. Magoo is totally out of touch with reality.

Unless somewhere in the mysterious depths of a Magoo's brain there lies a reality-perception seed that has not yet blossomed, his fate is irrevocably sealed. If he does possess such a dormant seed, there's always the hope that he can overcome the enormous odds against him and learn to correctly perceive and acknowledge reality. But if the seed has been undernourished and neglected for too long, the odds are against its ever sprouting. Of course, if such a seed doesn't exist to begin with, the Magoo's case is hopeless. About all you can do for such a person is offer him your condolences.

An Ostrich is an entirely different creature than a Mr. Magoo. The Ostrich has the mental capacity to correctly perceive reality, but stubbornly refuses to do so, preferring instead to live in a fantasy world of *ought to's*. Hard as it is to believe that anyone would make such a conscious choice, millions of people do so on a regular basis. The Ostrich is more tragic than the Mr. Magoo, because an individual who knows the facts but refuses to acknowledge them is the greatest of all fools. These are the kinds of fools we see so often on television, such as students and professors from some of our most prestigious centers of learning who harbor convoluted, incoherent ideas about such abstracts as "social justice" and saving the world. They may have a significant amount of knowledge, but their knowledge is corrupted by their misguided desire to recreate the world in their own image.

One note of caution: You should never confuse an Ostrich with The Liar. *Ought to's* are not The Liar's game. The Liar is a person who correctly perceives reality, but purposely attempts to hide it from others. In other words, he is sharply focused on purposeful deceit. As one might expect, one of the most prominent natural habitats of The Liar is to be found in the bowels of government.

With the exception of The Liar, then, when a person speaks of reality, what he is really referring to is *his* perception of reality. Everything that has ever been written, taught, or believed is based on someone's perception of reality. For example, everything in this book is based on my perception of reality. You are, of course, free to accept or reject any or all of my interpretations of reality. And where we have differences of opinion, one of us will suffer negative consequences to the degree to which his perceptions are incorrect. Conversely, to the degree either of us is correct in his perceptions of reality, his results will tend to be positive. But the one thing that will never be affected by our respective views of reality is reality itself.

THE REALITY OF RELATIVITY

Finally, an important reality of life that is too often forgotten: Virtually everything that happens to you is relative. To effectively deal with obstacles, you must first place them in proper perspective. If you allow any problem to be magnified beyond its merits, you're sure to have difficulty handling it in a rational manner.

In my early twenties, while stumbling around the streets of New York trying to promote a number of too-good-to-be-true deals, I developed an interesting relationship with an elderly, wealthy gentleman ("Harold Hart") who was a classic Lower East Side-to-Park Avenue success story. He had started out as a struggling, impoverished youth, but managed to amass a fortune by his early forties. He had it all—a chauffeured limousine to take him to and from Wall Street each day, an impeccable, expensive wardrobe, and a luxurious Park Avenue apartment decorated in Early Rich.

On several occasions, I had the opportunity to visit Mr. Hart at his home, and came to know him quite well. The purpose of my visits was to try to induce him to invest in some too-good-to-be-true venture, such as a sulfur mine in Tibet or gold-panning expedition in Tasmania. Though I consistently failed in my efforts to get him to part with any of his money, I obtained far more than I had bargained for in the form of knowledge and wisdom.

I vividly recall visiting Mr. Hart on one particular occasion when he was resting tranquilly in his favorite armchair. As usual, he was garbed in silk robe and pajamas, with servants waiting on him hand and foot. During the first few minutes of my visit, I recall observing the surreal scene as Mr. Hart sat quietly with a blank stare on his face. Then, without warning, he served up an unforgettable, philosophical tidbit to me.

In a barely audible monotone, Mr. Hart looked at me and said, "You know, nature has played a great hoax on man. All your life you strive to achieve success, you overcome endless obstacles and setbacks, you play all the silly little games that are required of you, and, if you're lucky, you finally make it to the top. Well, I made it to the top a long time ago, and you know what? It doesn't mean a damn thing. I tell you, nature has made a fool of man, and the biggest fool of all is me. Here I sit, in poor health, exhausted from years of playing the success game, knowing that time is running out, and I keep asking myself, 'Now what? What's your next clever move going to be?' The endless hours I spent working . . . worrying . . . maneuvering . . . negotiating—it was all for nothing. It's all so meaningless now, because, as I near the end, I realize that life is nothing more than a giant hoax. We think we're so important, but the truth is that we're nothing."

A few months after that cheerful little dissertation, I was informed that Harold Hart had passed away. That was many years ago, but today his words, and the tone in which he spoke them, still ring in my ears. Has nature made a fool of man? Is life just a big hoax? Though many years have passed since that memorable evening in his Park Avenue apartment, I still am not certain of the answers to these questions. However, even if life is not a

"How about a nice little sulfur mine in Tibet this evening?"

hoax—even if it is of universal importance—it does not necessarily follow that every problem we face is significant when juxtaposed against the endless complexities of the world, let alone the universe. The reality is that all problems are relative.

Nevertheless, some people react to a spilled cup of coffee with the same degree of stress that one would expect to experience when told that a terrorist attack is imminent. What such people lack is an understanding of the **Theory of Relativity**, which states: *In order to settle on a rational course of action (or inaction), one must first weigh all pertinent facts in a relative light and carefully define his terms.*

That you and I have problems is a given. The fundamental question is: problems relative to what?

Is middle age depressing you? In countries where the average life expectancy is forty, men and women are spared such depression.

Health problems? While any illness is disconcerting, the severity of a non-terminal illness must still be measured against the fatal medical conditions of untold millions of people worldwide.

Grocery bills getting you down? Hundreds of thousands of people die every day from starvation in Third World countries, while millions more suffer from malnutrition.

Unemployed? Relative to a person who lives in an underdeveloped country and has an annual income of $300, temporary unemployment in a Western country isn't all that serious of a problem.

Coping with the high cost of rent? Maybe you'd rather be a pavement dweller in Calcutta, India. These lucky people are born, live, and die on the pavement. The only thing they have to worry about is finding a rag to spread under their heads at night.

While these kinds of horrors continue along at their normal pace, we throw tantrums over being relegated to a poorly located table in our favorite restaurant, are frustrated because we can't seem to lose weight, and worry endlessly about money problems. It's all a result of the human tendency to be self-absorbed, a tendency that in turn makes it difficult for people to think about the pain and suffering of others.

Human dilemmas such as loneliness, financial problems, and government oppression at times overwhelm us. They prod some to drink, others to take drugs. They cause ulcers, migraine headaches, and high blood pressure. They can also produce stress and anxiety and precipitate serious mental and emotional disorders. The more your perspective is restricted to your own sheltered environment, the more likely you are to perceive minor difficulties as major problems. And when that occurs, it results in an unwarranted loss of finite time and energy.

Harkening back to Harold Hart's somber words on that unforgettable evening in his apartment reminds me that a person should make it a point to periodically step back and ask himself, "What if, in the overall scheme of things, my problems don't even matter? What if I'm allowing myself to become stressed and anxiety-ridden when, with just a slight reorientation of my perspective, I could experience tranquility and contentment?"

MACRO PROBLEMS

To place your problems in proper perspective, from time to time it's healthy to think about macro problems. By *macro problems*, I'm referring to potentially world-ending issues. Take, for example, overpopulation.

Barring outside interference, the population of a species increases in geometric proportions. Giving the majority of expert opinion the benefit of the doubt, this has resulted in man's proliferating to a population of about ten million in a span of somewhere between one to three million years (assuming you buy the Darwinian theory of evolution, at least to the extent you believe that today's man evolved from a humanoid that lived prior to the development of civilizations), then increasing his numbers to over six billion in just the next ten thousand years. In graphic mathematical terms, what this means is that the world's population is increasing at the rate of more than two people per second.

It is generally estimated that we will reach a world population of fourteen billion by the middle of this century (assuming, of course, that we make it that far). So where does it all end? Well, believe it or not, there is a limiting factor called *space*. Mathematicians tell us that if we continue at our present growth rate (2 percent per annum population increase), in about six hundred years the people then living will be faced with the rather awkward dilemma of having one individual for each square foot of land on our planet.

Some scientists believe that the solution is to colonize other planets. But is that really feasible? I recall reading an article many years ago by a physicist who was hypothesizing about a journey to another hospitable planet. He calculated that if a spaceship traveled at the speed of light, by the time it reached the nearest planet with environmental conditions resembling earth's (meaning, I assume, Big Mac wrappers lying on the sidewalks, strip centers on every block, etc.), the population of the spaceship (assuming it had departed with three people aboard) would equal the population of Planet Earth at the time of its departure!

What kind of time period am I talking about? Reaching just the planets in our own solar system would be a big enough problem. But it doesn't matter, because all of them have totally inhospitable temperatures and atmospheres anyway. Venus is enshrouded with sulfuric acid clouds, Mars's atmosphere approximates car exhaust, and Jupiter has been described as a giant sulfur and phosphorus match head. Given these antilife realities, it is highly unlikely that we will ever colonize another planet in our solar system.

How about other solar systems? Would you believe that the nearest star—repeat, *nearest*—Proxima Centauri, is 4.3 light years away? That's twenty-five *trillion* miles! What this means is that if we could build a spaceship capable of traveling at the speed of one million miles per hour, it would take six thousand years to make a round trip to our *closest* neighbor!

THE ULTIMATE PROBLEM SHRINKER

The greatest problem shrinker I've ever run across is the late exobiologist Carl Sagan's "cosmic calendar." As Sagan explained it,

"If the eons that comprise the lifetime of Earth were compressed into the span of a single year . . . recorded history would occupy the last thirty seconds of the last day of such a year."

Which means that the combined length of time it took to fight World War I and World War II, the Korean War, the Vietnam War, the Gulf War, and the Iraq War—which, by secular standards, were pretty serious problems—would occupy only a millifraction of a second in the lifetime of our planet. From this perspective, when someone shafts you in a business deal, does it really deserve the status of being able to give you a nervous breakdown? If you tried to squeeze such an event into Sagan's cosmic calendar, there wouldn't be a time measurement small enough to record it. To be sure, our everyday problems are real—and often frustrating and painful—but viewed from Sagan's cosmic-calendar perspective, few of them hardly deserve to be rated catastrophic.

Consider, for example, that in the late 1930s and early 1940s, Adolf Hitler, through virtual mass hypnosis, meted out morbid death sentences to more than six million innocent people. In Scarsdale, more than thirty years later, a descendant of one of those victims believes he is burdened by enormous difficulties. Someone at the office is vying for his position, his doctor has just informed him that he must give up smoking or face grave consequences, and his wife is threatening to leave him if he doesn't spend more time with his family. Yet, if this man were to be put in a time machine and found himself in Auschwitz in 1942, he would be incapable of identifying his future Scarsdale dilemmas as problems.

Likewise, if you were to find yourself in Hiroshima in the summer of 1945, I'd say you'd have a big problem. But if you were recently passed over for a promotion at work, it's not a world-ending event.

About three hundred years before Jesus appeared on earth, at a time when people's minds were not flooded by such serious concerns as who would win the NBA Finals, the World Series, or the Super Bowl, Taoist philosopher Chuang-tzu had time to reflect soberly on life:

> Once upon a time, I . . . dreamt I was a butterfly, flut-
> tering hither and thither, to all intents and purposes a
> butterfly. I was conscious only of following my fancies as
> a butterfly, and was unconscious of my individuality as
> a man. Suddenly I awoke, and there I lay, myself again.
> Now I do not know whether I was then a man dreaming
> that I was a butterfly, or whether I am now a butterfly
> dreaming that I am a man.

Just think, you're worrying yourself sick over unpaid bills, a mate who refuses to see things your way, a garage mechanic who pre-sents you with a bill that's a hundred dollars more than his original estimate, and for all you know you're nothing but a butterfly having a bad dream. Or maybe our whole universe is nothing more than a ping-pong ball that has fallen off a table in a world of giants. Worse, what if you and I happen to be living at a time when that ping-pong ball is about to hit the floor?

When you cut problems down to their true (i.e., relative) size, you will find them remarkably easier to handle. Is your greatest concern of the moment really all that important when placed against the circumstances of billions of people around the globe? Don't make the mistake of getting so caught up in your day-to-day problems that you are unable to view them in a relative light.

Most people carry far more baggage than necessary on their journey through life, and, like the airlines, nature charges us for excess baggage. But the odds are pretty good that you can't afford the cost of that baggage. Which is why you would be wise to lighten your load by reflecting on your problems in a relative light rather than pressure cooking them. Keep your troubles in proper perspective and master the art of taking them one step at a time.

With rational analysis, you may even find that many of your problems are not really problems at all. After all, we just use the word *problem* to refer to a fact or set of facts that we don't like. Whenever the word *problem* pops into your mind, you should quickly ask yourself, "Problem relative to what?" You must learn to view events in a relative light if you are to successfully make it over the Reality Hurdle.

UP AND OVER

It is of monumental importance to become adept at differentiating between reality and unreality, between fact and fiction, between what works and what doesn't work. Unfortunately, most people live in a totally *unreal* world. As discussed earlier, they create a world in their own minds based on the way they would *like* the world to be rather than the way it actually *is*. They would much rather delude themselves by ignoring the facts, even if their self-delusion only prolongs the inevitable.

While the development of a correct perception of reality is not an easy task, due in no small part to our being surrounded by a world of delusions, the nice thing about it is that anyone can get better with practice—*provided* he is committed to truth. Which means being willing to subordinate your desires and wishes—your dreams, as it were—to reality. That is not to say you should not have dreams. On the contrary, dreams can provide the fuel for persevering. However, you should never allow your dreams and desires to be so all-consuming that they repress reality. Put another way, your love of truth must be greater than your desire to make your dreams come true.

In a free country, of course, you have a right to go on believing whatever you want to believe. But, at the same time, you should recognize that reality is not discriminatory. Meaning that nature does not accept ignorance as an excuse for making wrong decisions. It metes out negative consequences just as harshly to a person who is well-meaning but misinformed as to someone who is malevolent and stubborn. Not once has reality excused anyone for good motives, so consistency is essential when it comes to having a proper perception of reality.

The nice thing about reality is that you do have a choice. You can choose to accept reality and use it to your benefit or you can ignore it and allow it to create havoc in your life. A wise person makes a serious effort to avoid the pitfall of confusing the way he believes things ought to be with the way they really are. Never be so afraid of truth that you refuse to acknowledge it. How are you to deal effectively with the facts if you deny their existence?

When you correctly perceive reality, delusions begin to disappear. And as delusions vanish from your life, you are able to deal more effectively with problems on a rational basis, which in turn leads to long-term success.

3 The Intimidation Hurdle

Without being consciously aware of it, a large percentage of our day-to-day actions are motivated by fear. For example, you can be motivated by the fear of physical harm, the fear of losing a business deal, or the fear of being embarrassed. While such fears may sometimes be well founded, often they are just a result of being intimidated, because intimidation is motivation through fear.

In order to recognize when you're being intimidated, you have to familiarize yourself with the many ways in which intimidation is camouflaged. Whenever you suspect that you might have inadvertently gotten trapped into playing the role of the intimidatee, ask yourself a simple question: Why am I doing what I'm doing? If you can trace the reason for your actions to motivation through fear, no matter how subtle it may be, then intimidation is the culprit. All too often we react like Pavlovian dogs and obey

31

the commands of others without stopping to analyze why. Actions based on intimidation can become such an accepted mode of behavior that we reach a point where we don't even recognize the true source of our motivation.

Of course, there will always be self-righteous, professional halo-wearers who become indignant at the mere mention of the word *intimidation*. Whenever you run into such holier-than-thou characters, you should be vigilant about refusing to allow them to throw you off guard. It's been my experience that those who protest the loudest about the evils of intimidation are the very people who most frequently employ it. Given that human beings are masters at self-delusion, many high-level intimidators sincerely believe they are saints. But whether or not someone admits—even to himself—that he uses intimidation as a tool is irrelevant. If the shoe fits, it fits.

INTIMIDATION THROUGH WEALTH

Wealth can give an otherwise inept person a strong—even overwhelming—posture. To psychologically defend yourself against such a person, you should keep in mind that another individual's net worth does not dilute your own intrinsic value. Money should be respected, but never overrated. Make the other person come up with something more than a good balance sheet before conceding an inch of ground to him. There is no requirement for you to grant him permission to have power over you. What you bring to the table could very well be worth far more than the other guy's money.

INTIMIDATION THROUGH CREDENTIALS

What is an expert? All too often, he's just someone who can tell you all the reasons why you can't do something. Personally, I prefer to discover for myself what I am or am not capable of accomplishing. Sometimes an expert is nothing more than an ordinary guy from out of town who knows his job. I have always marveled at how an individual's expert status seems to increase in direct proportion to the distance between his current place of residence and his hometown.

The printed word helps to create experts, too. For years I was saying many of the same things I now write about in books, but I didn't attract too many listeners. I don't want to make you feel bad, but if you had been around me during those times, you could have gotten most of the information in this book for free. In fact, I probably would have treated you to lunch just for listening to me.

Some years ago, a director and an instructor in psychiatry, both from the University of Southern California Medical School, teamed up with an assistant professor of medical education at Southern Illinois University to conduct an unusual experiment. They arranged to have a Dr. Myron L. Fox, purportedly an authority on the application of mathematics to human behavior, speak to a group of fifty-five educators, school administrators, psychiatrists, psychologists, and social workers. His topic was "mathematical game theory as applied to physician education."

Forty-two of the fifty-five people in attendance agreed that the speaker's examples helped to clarify the subject and that the material was well organized and the lecture stimulating. Which was fine, except for the fact that Dr. Fox was a hired actor and his lecture was never meant to be anything but pure double-talk!

At best, experts are people who are knowledgeable in their fields—knowledgeable, but not infallible—and the best ones will openly admit it. As specialists, they tend to suffer from myopia. To paraphrase the great logotherapist Viktor Frankl, an expert is often nothing more than a person who cannot see the forest of truth for the trees of facts.

THE CERTIFICATE

An expert with a certificate on his wall is in a strong position to be a intimidator, but only if you allow yourself to become enamored by his expert credentials. Just because someone has a license from the government, a university, or any other institution that allows him to practice his profession without having to worry about unlicensed competition (a phenomenon known in organized crime as "protection racket") doesn't mean he has all the answers.

No diploma, license, or other piece of paper can take the place of knowledge and ability. In this regard, your attitude toward self-anointed experts should be: Don't try to overwhelm me with your diplomas or years of experience; instead, impress me with your knowledge and demonstrable results.

If you're accustomed to checking out a person's certification credentials for confirmation of his expertise, particularly if his only credential is a piece of paper issued by some bureaucratic institution, best you break that naïve habit as quickly as possible. Then get *in* the habit of checking a person's premises when he speaks. If his premises are sound, only then does it make sense to consider—not blindly accept—what he has to say.

A classic example of intimidating credentials can be seen in medical doctors. Is there anything more irritating than a doctor who rushes you through your examination, talks down to you, and gives you flip answers? If you remain in a relationship with such a doctor, it can lead to serious consequences, not the least of which is unnecessary surgery. Never agree to undergo an invasive procedure without first obtaining at least one other professional opinion.

If that hurts your doctor's feelings, he's the wrong doctor for you. Your doctor may have good intentions every time someone walks through his office door, but the reality is that he isn't as concerned about your welfare as you are. He might be the most ethical and qualified physician in the world, but the fact is that you are just one of many patients he sees every day. He may be a medical doctor, but he's also human, which makes it impossible for him to have the same degree of interest in your health as you do.

Never forget that in *your* life, *you* are the main event. And if you lose the main event, you don't get another chance. True, you can't take matters completely into your own hands when it comes to medicine, because you obviously can't perform surgery on yourself.

But there's nothing to stop you from obtaining a second, or even third, qualified opinion when a doctor hands down an ominous diagnosis. Because doctors are human, they're entitled to make mistakes. Just make certain that you don't end up being on the wrong end of one of the more serious mistakes your doctor may make. If you aren't vigilant in this area, looking out for number one can quickly become a moot point.

If you haven't already done so, it would be much to your benefit to develop the self-discipline to avoid making decisions based solely on the opinions of purported experts. By all means, listen to what the experts have to say, but be certain to weigh what you hear against all other available evidence. Above all, weigh it against your reasoning power, then make decisions accordingly.

Whenever you start to relapse into allowing yourself to be intimidated by experts, remember that the great Greek philosopher Aristotle once insisted that the earth was the center of the universe and that seven planets—which he believed included the sun and the moon—revolved around it. Based on scientific knowledge available at that time, his pronouncements were perfectly reasonable. The problem is that new evidence in virtually every field emerges almost daily, which all too often makes last year's experts look rather foolish. Hey, if you can't trust Aristotle, who *can* you trust? The good news is that no expert can hold your mind captive against your will.

INTIMIDATION THROUGH CUSTOM AND TRADITION

Intimidation through custom and tradition can affect many areas of a person's life and play havoc with his reasoning powers. It runs the gamut from law and religion to protocol at social gatherings to the proper setting of a dinner table.

Human beings have been known to be a bit overzealous when it comes to protecting the status quo. In the strictest sense of the word, most people are conservative in that they lean toward preserving existing conditions, feeling safer with established customs.

This ingrained fear of change can cause people to resort to their irrational worst in defense of their protected monopolies.

When it comes to custom and tradition, people tend to spend a great deal of time and energy doing things for which they hope to be appreciated. It's nice when it happens, but it's a big mistake to base your actions on the desire to gain the gratitude of others, as spelled out in the **You-Won't-Get-Credit-for-It Theory**, which states: *Never do anything with the expectation of being appreciated. The most valid reason for taking an action is that you sincerely want to do it.*

Often, when we yield to peer or societal pressure and do something just because it's "the right thing to do," we are surprised and disappointed to discover that people not only do not appreciate what we've done, but may even dislike us for it. A good example of this is when you begrudgingly tip a waiter who has given you bad service. Because it's an established custom to leave tips in restaurants, when a waiter serves you cold food, makes you wait twenty minutes for a glass of water, and snarls at you for asking a question, you may find yourself torn over whether or not to leave him a tip.

Unfortunately, notwithstanding such terrible service, the fear of feeling embarrassed might overrule your reasoning powers and motivate you to leave a tip anyway. But in an attempt to file at least a mild protest against the waiter, you decide to tip him a little less than the standard 15–20 percent. *Zap!* Custom and tradition has intimidated you into making an irrational decision for which you won't get credit. Instead, what you *will* get is a triple loss: 1) You didn't enjoy your meal because of the bad service; 2) the waiter scorns you for leaving him less of a tip than he expected (and— insult of all insults—may even disrespect you for not having the courage to refuse to tip him at all); and 3) you're out the money you did leave him as a tip!

In the ancient language of hieroglyphics, you're what is commonly known as a *J-E-R-K*. But, take heart. If you dine out often enough, the money you save in tips during the next year alone as a result of employing the You-Won't-Get-Credit-for-It Theory should pay for the cost of this book many times over.

"Thanks for the tip, jerk. Are you sure you can afford it?"

Common sense tells us that if a belief was irrational or immoral when it first came into existence, it doesn't become any more rational or moral with the passage of time. The seniority of a custom bears no relationship whatsoever to its rational or moral validity. Those who revere long-standing customs merely because of their entrenchment are living their lives on shaky ground—morally, philosophically, and rationally.

If an established practice works well for you and does not harm others, that's fine. But practices that have no bases in fact, whose premises rest on quicksand, should be discarded. If past ideas contradict reality, logic, or current circumstances, they should be abandoned without ceremony. It takes nothing more than common sense and courage to eliminate long-standing, irrational customs or traditions.

Since looking out for number one requires an awareness of what you're doing and why you're doing it, it's incumbent upon you to rid yourself of customs and traditions that are either irrational, immoral, or both. Regardless of how old or how well accepted a custom or tradition may be, it is obliged to stand the test of time and changing circumstances.

INTIMIDATION THROUGH CONFORMITY

Intimidation through conformity is a first cousin to intimidation through custom and tradition. When you're intimidated into going along with a new fad, a new idea that has gained wide acceptance, or the latest "in" thing, you are conforming. Whenever you find yourself doing something just because everybody else is doing it, your action is motivated by the fear of standing apart from the herd. As every concerned parent knows, teenagers are especially prone to such misguided actions.

Just because something is in vogue doesn't make it good or bad. It only means that more people are doing it, wearing it, or saying it. But if you rationally decide upon a different course of action, that doesn't make you inferior, stupid, or weird. All it means is that you're comfortable enough with who you are to base your actions on your own independent thinking.

THE THOUSANDUPLETS

Speaking of standing apart from the herd, in the seventies, when I was single and living in Los Angeles, I once took a drive down to Manhattan Beach to survey the social situation I had heard so much about. As I trudged across the sand toward one of the volleyball nets, vigorously sucking my thumb and performing dazzling loop-the-loops with my yo-yo, I became puzzled. It was like a weird dream, as though I had landed on a faraway planet.

There, in Manhattan Beach, I saw them: the Thousanduplets. It seemed there were a thousand identical twins standing around with cans of Bud Light in their right hands. Each of the Thousanduplets was tall and displayed six-pack abs, a dark tan, and well-coiffed, bleached-blond hair. Cocked at just the right angle at the front of their blond mops were sunglasses, the kind no one ever wears over his eyes. It wasn't a commercial. It was real life. These guys were actually concentrating on assuming cool poses—and, of course, making sure their sunglasses didn't fall off. And the girls around them were neither pretty nor smiling like the ones you see in those TV ads.

I found this scene to be not only perplexing, but depressing. Even if I were able to balance a pair of sunglasses at the top of my forehead, I could never hope to fit in. My hair wasn't blond, my stomach wasn't flat and rippled, I didn't drink beer, and there was no way I could ever tan my tortoise shell. As I made my way back to my car, I looked over my shoulder to catch one last glimpse of the Thousanduplets, did a final loop-the-loop with my yo-yo, and thought to myself, "Amazing . . . really amazing."

What an anonymous life, that of the Thousanduplet. Many unanswered questions still haunt me. Like what kind of woman gave birth to a thousand boys? How do they know they're in the right apartment at night? And if their sunglasses should fall off and break, are they exiled to Redondo Beach? If reality TV had been in vogue back then, I'm convinced I could have sold the idea to one of

"Amazing . . . really amazing."

the major networks. I can see it now: *The Trials and Tribulations of the Thousanduplets.* Each week, one bikini-clad movie star wannabe would have romantic interludes with a number of Thousanduplets, then ultimately pick the one she believed had the most awesome abs, the darkest tan, the blondest, best-coiffed hair, and the biggest unemployment check.

The herd instinct in all of us makes conforming feel natural, but the fact is that conforming may not be in your long-term best interest. With time, you will discover that people will admire you more for having the courage to do what you think is right, even though they may chide or admonish you in the short term. Any parent who can get a teenager to understand this reality deserves to be in the Parent Hall of Fame.

Tenaciously resist the inclination to do something just because it's in style. While it may seem like the easiest thing to do at the time, it can be far too costly over the long term. Conforming, as the channel of least resistance, can carry a heavy price tag—the loss of one's self-respect.

INTIMIDATION THROUGH SLOGAN

By *slogan*, I am referring to any phrase, saying, or adage—new or old—intended to effect a knee-jerk response from listeners. Whether the intended purpose of the slogan is good or bad by your standards, a slogan is irrational to the extent one tries to use it as a basis for getting others to stop doing something they are doing or to do something they don't want to do. Slogans are an effective tool for keeping others in line, especially when used by Absolute Moralists. Consider such slogans as:

War Is Peace
Freedom Is Slavery
Ignorance Is Strength

You may recognize the above words as Big Brother's slogan in George Orwell's all-too-real novel *1984*. It is intended to be the definitive irrational slogan. Orwell was making the point that people can be made to believe just about anything if they hear it often enough. Through slogans backed by traditional government force, all citizens in *1984* are kept in line, conforming to the point where they are virtually mindless, ready to accept any slogan as fact.

In real life, "doublespeak" is a powerful tool used by governments to convince the masses that hell is paradise via a never-ending stream of clouded and twisted phrases and slogans, such as "shared prosperity," "the good of society," and "fair share." Governments are masters of intimidation through slogan, and they have the money, the manpower, and, if needed, the guns to back up their slogans.

The bottom line is that you should never allow yourself to be intimidated by a slogan. A slogan, of and by itself, is not a valid reason for taking action, particularly if such action results in pain or discomfort. More often than not, the real purpose of a slogan is to try to intimidate you into helping the slogan maker advance his own agenda. Be vigilant about not buying into it. A rational person bases his behavior on facts.

INTIMIDATION THROUGH GUILT

Guilt is a state of mind you need not endure. Within the boundaries of a generally accepted code of conduct, you and you alone must decide what is right and wrong for you. And once you've done so, there is no reason to feel guilty for acting in a manner considered improper by someone else's standards.

In this regard, beware the Absolute Moralist, the shameless meddler we unmasked in Chapter 1. Because he is convinced that his view of morality is right for everyone, the Absolute Moralist is able to justify just about any action he deems necessary to convert others to his beliefs. Consequently, he shackles himself with no restraints when it comes to meddling in the lives of others. The Absolute Moralist is a master at inducing guilt feelings aimed at intimidating people into seeing things his way.

Self-righteous individuals are also master guilt inducers. (All Absolute Moralists are self-righteous people, but not all self-righteous people are Absolute Moralists.) Those who are obsessively focused on claiming the moral high ground possess monstrous egos. However, what you see and what you get when dealing with a self-righteous person can be quite different. Be wary of the individual who states his virtuous case in such a way as to make you feel guilty for not being up to his moral standards.

There is no end to the number of guilt games people play. Given an opening, there are individuals who will gladly criticize and blame you for everything from losing their jobs to passing up opportunities for better jobs. Overcoming the fear of being condemned for refusing to do what others want you to do requires a great deal of self-discipline. Never accept a responsibility just because someone thinks you should. An important step in clearing the Intimidation Hurdle is to understand the wisdom contained in the **No Theory**, which states: *Learn to say no politely and pleasantly, but immediately and firmly.* Simple to say, but often difficult to do.

Again, morality is a very personal matter, and, as such, you should not allow others to decide your moral code for you. Make the foundational decisions regarding your own moral standards, then refuse to allow another person's opinion on the subject to evoke feelings of guilt. Because that's just what it will be—*someone else's* opinion.

Also, don't be so willing to accept criticism and blame, and, whether or not it's justified, don't waste time feeling guilty about it. If you engage in behavior that you later decide was wrong by *your* standards, guilt is not the solution. Instead, make the necessary apology, in a straightforward manner, *one time*—then forget about it. On the other hand, if you're not guilty, skip the apology and just forget about it.

You are a human being, and, as such, you should accept the fact that, like everyone else on this planet, you sometimes make mistakes. Even if your mistake can be classified as major, feeling guilty about it will do absolutely nothing to rectify the situation.

By all means, strive to learn from your mistake, then let go of it and pledge to be vigilant about not repeating it.

You have no need to feel guilty for looking out for number one, and to the extent you allow other people to sap your energy by engendering guilt, you will be moving away from that noble objective. Also, don't forget that it cuts both ways, so make certain you do not attempt to induce guilt feelings in others.

INTIMIDATION THROUGH SLANDER

If you can keep your head when all about you
Are losing theirs and blaming it on you . . .

If you don't understand your accuser's neuroses, slander can be a very intimidating tool. Since all human beings possess, to varying degrees, such negative traits as jealousy, envy, hatred, and cruelty, slander is widely used for venting emotions.

If you can bear to hear the truth you've spoken
Twisted by knaves to make a trap for fools . . .

When someone tries to twist your words, change your meanings, or restate your intentions, you may instinctively feel like lashing out and defending yourself. There's a natural inclination to want to prove to the world that what has been said about you is false. Everything else becomes secondary to righting the terrible wrong that has been committed against you. And once your emotions reach that point, the slanderer has won!

Why would someone have a desire to slander you? There could be any number of reasons. He may envy you because of your achievements; he may be frustrated over his own low station in life; or he may be unfortunate enough to possess such traits as envy and/or cruelty to an excessive degree. Whatever his reasons, the moment you begin analyzing your critic's intentions, you've already taken a step in the wrong direction. Recognize that it's *his* problem, not yours. Then simply ignore his remarks.

Or being hated, don't give way to hating . . .

Hatred can be jarring to an individual who generally minds his own business and is focused on his own affairs. There is so much bitterness in our world due to feelings of inadequacy, guilt, and failure—not to mention perceived self-sacrifice—that the neurotic individual often feels that he can vent his frustration only through hatred.

Or being lied about, don't deal in lies . . .

Perhaps the most difficult type of slander to swallow is the outright lie. It's like being shocked with a cattle prod. When it strikes, it throws you off balance, often leaving you stunned and speechless.

What is most difficult about an out-and-out lie is the depressing reality that there will always be some people who will believe it, and others who will at least partially believe it. The tendency to give credence to even the most outrageous lie is based on the old adage that "where there's smoke, there's fire"—which is precisely what makes slander such an effective weapon.

Fortunately, the effects of a lie are usually short-lived, even among irrational people, provided you don't make the mistake of helping to keep the lie in the spotlight. The less you say, the better, because rational people view a lie in the same way they view any other kind of statement not supported by facts.

The reality is that you are going to be slandered from time to time, so you shouldn't allow it to throw you into a state of emotional turmoil when it happens. If you feel the necessity to defend yourself against a lie, the best approach is to first give yourself time to cool off and think the matter through rationally. During the cooling-off period, try your best to analyze the facts with a dispassionate mind-set. Then, after you've thought it through carefully, state your defense clearly, simply, and firmly, but only to those whose opinions you value. Avoid nasty adjectives and broad-sweeping statements that only succeed in discrediting you. Skip the extraneous and forego repetition. The destruction of the lie in the eyes of those you care about will very much depend upon how *you* handle the matter.

It's not a matter of turning the other cheek. It's a matter of doing what's in your best interest. To feel compelled to expose a lie to every person you come across is counterproductive. In any event, an overly vehement defense rarely convinces others that the slander is not true. On the contrary, the louder the protest, the more suspicious it tends to make people. An important rule to remember when dealing with people in all areas of life is: The power of the understatement is enormous.

INTIMIDATION THROUGH GROUPING AND TAGGING

Human beings have a habit of creating fictitious entities to describe large numbers of individuals. "Government," "the people," and "society" are classic examples of this. They are abstract terms that refer to groups of people, and groups do not have qualities. Only people do. So, while every individual within a group possesses human traits, the group itself does not.

When you stamp a person with a group label or tag, you not only are being unfair to him, but to yourself. You are cheating yourself of what that person, as a unique human being, has to offer. Tagging people is a convenient tool that makes it easier to indulge irrational hatreds. When you combine bigotry with slander, you have the most irrational and dangerous of all weapons. Those who suffer from a lack of self-esteem need scapegoats, because if they can vent their anger on others, they need not search within for the true cause of their lack of self-esteem.

There has always been prejudice in the world, and you can be certain there always will be. The word *barbarian* has been traced all the way back to Sanskrit, where it translates as "stammerer." The idea was that if a person didn't speak your language and act like you, he was a stammerer—an ignoramus.

Since there wasn't much contact in the early centuries between different races, most bigotry was based on religion. You weren't a man—you were a Jew, a Christian, or a heathen. Then again, you may have been a woman, which automatically saddled you with a number of traits you may not have possessed. Aristotle insisted that women had inconclusive reasoning powers, and that their nature was, for the most part, inferior. In his judgment, "A man would be thought a coward who had no more courage than a courageous woman."

As centuries passed and the world grew smaller, the opportunities for coming in contact with human beings with different physical characteristics increased. And though millions of people still clung to irrational methods of grouping and tagging, the phenomenon of differing skin color made scapegoating much easier, especially for people with feelings of inferiority.

As early as 1758, Carl Von Linne, the famous Swedish botanist, made the characteristics of all black people accepted scientific fact. In working out a system of classifying every known living being, which actually became a cornerstone for modern biology, Linne "scientifically" described the black African as "crafty, indolent, negligent, and governed by caprice." With science on its side, racism gained an air of respectability.

Later, in the United States, all sorts of irrational actions continued to reaffirm Linne's scientific judgment. In 1857, Chief Justice Taney of the Supreme Court, in handing down the famed Dred Scott decision, reasoned that a black person "has no rights which a white man need respect."

Abraham Lincoln, in one of his well-publicized debates with Stephen Douglas, stated: "I am not nor ever have been in favor of bringing about in any way the social and political equality of the white and black races ... there must be the position of superior and inferior, and I as much as any other man am in favor of having the superior position assigned to the white race."

But this kind of grouping wasn't reserved for blacks. If you were different from the majority of the population, you qualified as a faceless, brainless member of a group. President Theodore Roosevelt once exclaimed, "I don't go so far as to think that the only good Indians are dead Indians, but I believe nine out of every ten are, and I shouldn't inquire too closely into the case of the tenth. The most vicious cowboy has more moral principle than the average Indian."

While it's fine to be proud of your heritage, you should also recognize that you had nothing to do with the actions of your ancestors. In fact, you never even knew them. What your ancestors accomplished is no feather in your cap, nor should you feel responsible for their sins. The real issue is how you live *your* life and what *you* have accomplished. Be proud of who you are. If your great-grandfather was a rapist or horse thief, that would not affect my opinion of you. (Of course, if he was a criminal-defense attorney, that might be another matter.)

Make it a point never to take an irrational stand against someone because of his race, religion, or any other irrelevant characteristic out of fear that you may not be accepted by your peers. If your peers don't accept those who refuse to play the grouping-and-tagging game, the solution is not to appease them but to find new peers. Don't be intimidated by those who would try to place you in a cookie-cutter category, and make certain that *you* are never guilty of grouping or tagging others.

EXORCISING INVALID FEARS

The various kinds of intimidation I have discussed in this chapter are but a small sampling of the ways in which people can be motivated to take action through fear. Some fears are valid, but most are not, and it's the invalid fears that should be exorcised from your life. And the key to accomplishing that is to constantly ask yourself the question, "Why am I doing what I'm doing?"

Whenever the answer is *fear*, the second step is to analyze whether or not your fear is valid. If so (e.g., someone might literally be holding a gun to your head), by all means do what needs to be done to make the best of a bad situation, but nothing more; i.e., keep your emotions under control. But if your fear is irrational, shift gears and employ your intellect to decide on a correct course of action. You've crossed the Intimidation Hurdle when you are able to make such course corrections quickly and consistently.

4 The Crusade Hurdle

By *crusade* (used interchangeably in this chapter with the word *cause*), I am referring to the platform of any group, regardless of its purported objectives, that calls for aggressive action to advance an idea or eliminate an existing idea or circumstance. Perhaps you are presently involved in such a group, though you may not have thought about it as a crusade.

I am not against the existence of causes per se, because everyone certainly has a right to pursue whatever interests he so desires so long as he does not commit aggression against others in the process. Further, I would have to concede that many causes have noble objectives, the best examples of which are private charities whose financial records are open to the general public. Most causes, however, are not noble. Worse, many use aggressive tactics to such an extreme that they are a menace to peaceful individuals who just want to be left alone.

There is a seemingly endless supply of proclaimed good causes one can support, so the first problem is to figure out which one or ones to join. Some of the better-known causes we hear about almost daily involve debates about "climate change," saving endangered species, preservation of the earth's rain forests, pornography on the Internet, racial profiling, legalization of drugs, pro-choice vs pro-life, euthanasia, gay marriage, gun control, and special rights for the handicapped, elderly, illegal immigrants, and numerous other groups.

The Diaper Corps (all people under twenty-five years of age and those over thirty who still play with rattles) is responsible for many of the most absurd movements we hear about almost daily. Were such movements not given publicity by the media, most of their would-be causes would undoubtedly die swiftly. Young people are amazingly flexible. They can be militant about the environment one day, socialism the next, then—who knows?—the merits of mating mice with giraffes.

One of the most disturbing things about crusades is that they tend to become ends in themselves. The official objective of the group somehow gets lost in the rearranging of the facts, the endless bureaucracy of its corporate structure, and the never-ending bashing of its foes. With all this going on, the crusade never quite seems to get around to its stated purpose. That's why the all-or-nothing approach is usually favored; i.e., you must accept *all* tenets of the group, no questions asked. Mass-movement leaders throughout history have been well aware that outside interests detract from the energies needed to keep a movement going full steam.

Whether a crusade is created by the Diaper Corps or irrational adults, its true value should be judged on the basis of logic, reality, and fact. And even if its stated purpose passes the test of reason, a movement is still unjustified if it interferes with the lives of nonmembers. An unsound crusade of any kind is a major hurdle that can complicate your life in numerous ways, and avoiding such complications begins with understanding that the concept of group action is fundamentally unsound.

THE COOKIE-CUTTER PHENOMENON

One of the most fascinating things about crusades is that no matter what their members purport to believe in, their structures are remarkably similar. Throughout history, the nature of crusades may have changed, but their basic characteristics have remained intact. Some of the more common components of virtually all crusades are described below.

GROUPING AND TAGGING WITH AN OFFICIAL STAMP

All crusades put labels on individuals, which is reason enough to avoid them. But, unlike general grouping and tagging, crusades are puffed up in stature by the use of official-sounding names. A common cause, whether rational or irrational, unites those involved, which sounds relatively harmless on the surface. The problem is that it erroneously assumes that just because you support a cause, its leader speaks on your behalf—which means you involuntarily lose your individuality the moment you take part in group action.

Organizations themselves would be irrelevant to nonmembers if they did not undertake crusades. To use a hypothetical example, a tennis club is a perfectly harmless group so long as its members stick to playing tennis with one another. But if they suddenly decide it's their duty to make everyone in the world play tennis, then embark on a campaign to solicit new members through pressure tactics, the tennis club is transformed into a tennis *crusade*.

Though the above example may sound a bit farfetched, it is precisely how a seemingly harmless group transforms itself into a crusade. It all starts when members of the group begin to interfere in the lives of others by pressuring them to join or by attempting to force them to do, or not do, something that will bring their actions in line with the group's objectives. And that's the point at which the group threatens to become a dangerous obstacle to your happiness.

You should steadfastly refuse to relinquish your individuality to any group of people just because it happens to have a particular characteristic in common with you, whether it be sex, skin color, religious affiliation, or occupation. Be careful about allowing such people to refer to you as "one of us."

You should insist on remaining an individual and showing the world what you, as a unique entity, have to offer. It is dangerous to accept the blanket characteristics of any group. If you're a woman, you're different than any other woman in the world; if you're an elderly person, there is no other elderly person exactly like you; if your skin color is brown, there isn't another brown person in existence with the same traits you possess. Plain and simple, if you're a human being, you're a one of a kind, which is why you should never allow the Crusade Hurdle to become a barrier between you and your efforts to demonstrate your uniqueness to the world.

DISTORTION

Virtually every movement excels in the distortion or deletion of relevant information. Those promoting a crusade quite naturally paint only their side of the picture, so one should not be particularly impressed with the seeming worthiness of any cause or the reasonableness of any group's sales pitch. More often than not, such a sales pitch is based on false premises, so it is incumbent on you to challenge all premises. Also, remember that figures *do* lie. Some figures bandied about by crusaders are just plain false, so never make the mistake of assuming what you hear is correct just because the information is in print or is given in an authoritative manner. And even when figures are correct, they can still be used out of context to cleverly make one's case.

EMPHASIS ON THE FUTURE

Not only are the motivations for becoming involved in most causes questionable, but causes rarely achieve their stated goals. In fact, if causes had to rely on their track records alone, they would find it much more difficult to attract supporters. The most obvious examples of this are crusades to end war and poverty. Judging from 6,000 years of recorded history, poverty would appear to be a natural consequence of the ebb and flow of human events, particularly those related to government capriciousness.

Poverty is a subjective condition, but we can certainly all agree that extreme forms of poverty are found only where the most tyrannical forms of government exist. When people are free to pursue their own interests, wealth is created in the process. In so-called democratic countries, no one who is willing to work is poor in the Third World sense of the word.

As to peace movements, short of self-styled saviors conquering every country on earth and holding in check those with aspirations to invade other countries, world peace is not possible. Crusaders can preach peace to their heart's content, but their words will have no effect whatsoever on the next Hugo Chavez, Osama bin Laden, or Mahmoud Ahmadinejad. And for every malevolent individual who today holds the reins of power, there are thousands of individuals as bad, or worse, waiting in the wings for the opportunity to grab those reigns.

Given these realities, an emphasis on the future has been an important tool of crusaders for centuries. So long as success is projected far into the future, dedication to the cause can be justified. The less a movement offers in the present and the more it offers in the future, the better its chances of success. Most crusades would fizzle out rather quickly if they promised immediate results. So if you intend to start a movement of your own, I would suggest that you give your enlistees a far-out target date for achieving the crusade's objectives. The year 2140 might be a nice date to shoot for. If you can sell them on a date far enough into the future, you may be able to keep your members in line throughout your lifetime.

ORGANIZATION

Critical to the success of crusades is the degree to which they are corporately organized. The better the planning and structure of a group, the more it gives the illusion of being a living entity. That, in turn, makes it easier to strip its followers of their individuality. Individual characteristics, after all, pose a threat to the group's purported objective—meaning the objective of its leader—so the better organized the movement, the more awed its members are likely to be.

THE DEVIL

Most mass movements find it necessary to create a devil. If there is a crusade to "preserve the coastline," the devil is the individual who doesn't want his beach property confiscated for the "public good." If it's a crusade to increase "corporate responsibility," the devil is the corporate executive. "Heretics" were the Inquisition's devil; Jews were Hitler's devil; and today, America and Israel comprise the big and little devils for much of the Arab world. If no other devil is convenient, a group leader will settle for just about anyone who doesn't belong to his movement. The good guys are those involved; the bad guys are those who haven't yet "seen the light."

THE USE OF FORCE

Perhaps the most irrational aspect of all when it comes to getting involved in a cause is that many of them resort to force to achieve their ends. What actually happens in most cases is that crusaders appeal to the government to force people to act in accordance with their desires. Often, this aggression comes in the form of lobbying government officials for special rights (i.e., pressuring politicians to pass new laws to help them achieve their objectives, knowing that the power holders have the guns and manpower to make certain these objectives-turned-laws will be enforced), and special rights for some always violate the rights of others. Whenever a group is formed for the purpose of inducing politicians to create a new law, what it really amounts to, when stripped of its slogans and pretenses, is appealing to the government to impose the group's personal beliefs on others.

Though most people have strong beliefs about one or more causes, such beliefs represent nothing more than personal opinions, and, as such, are morally inferior to individual liberty. If people are serious about living in a free society, liberty must be given a higher priority than all other objectives, including any and all causes that certain people may deem to be noble.

Unfortunately, there will always be misguided individuals who arrogantly believe that achieving their desired objectives justifies virtually any means. This is especially true of those who sermonize about world peace, the environment, eradication of poverty, or such abstracts as "social justice" and "shared prosperity." All too often, the endgame for the leader of a cause is repression of individual freedom. As Nobel Prize novelist and poet Anatole France so rightly pointed out, "Those who have given themselves the most concern about the happiness of peoples have made their neighbors very miserable."

Relying on persuasion to take something from others or to force people to do something they don't want to do is a difficult proposition. A well-organized crusade makes it much easier and safer to violate the rights of others via the threat of government force. Hiding behind the strong arm of government blurs the reality that such interference is being perpetrated by one's neighbors. If members perceive that an abstract entity—"the group"—is committing aggression, they can morally justify it by contending that it benefits "society as a whole."

You should refuse to relinquish your individuality under pressure from any group whose members might all happen to desire a similar social change. And if a group's intention is to bring about social change through the threat of government force, that, of and by itself, is an excellent reason not to become involved. The use of force for anything other than self-defense is *never* morally justified.

SLOGANS

The deployment of slogans is another common denominator of most movements. As a general rule, the less a slogan actually says (think "hope and change"), the greater its appeal. Slogans are employed because to the unthinking individual they appear on the surface to be interchangeable with fact. "Love it or leave it" makes it a fact that the country belongs to those making the statement and that you are under an obligation either to agree with their political views or move to another country. The more clever the slogan, the less the crusader need concern himself with facts.

THE SPECTACLE

"The Spectacle" goes hand in hand with slogans when it comes to stirring the emotions of crusade members. From the smallest protest march to the most elaborate parade or ceremony, spectacles are an essential element of most crusades, so much so that they often can be the glue that holds together a shaky structure that would otherwise crumble. When reality threatens to shatter a group member's faith, a spectacular ritual, however meaningless, can be the ideal antidote for keeping him in line.

Political rallies are perfect examples of this phenomenon, with balloons and confetti falling from the ceiling, music blaring, and intellectually comatose people laughing, shouting, and wildly thrusting VOTE FOR signs into the air. Ditto with military parades before, during, and after a war. The greater the spectacle, the more effective it is likely to be. The spectacle is an escape from reality, a vehicle for pretending.

PROFILE OF A CRUSADE LEADER

The prototype of a crusade leader may not seem very different from that of other neurotics who have stumbled into your life over the years, but the one characteristic you can always count on is an insatiable ego. The crusade leader believes he can save the world by imposing his will on others. Rest assured, however, that if his own life were more meaningful, his burning conviction for his cause would be radically diminished. As Eric Hoffer pointed out, "A man is likely to mind his own business when it is worth minding. When it is not, he takes his mind off his own meaningless affairs by minding other people's business."

The leaders of so-called mass movements, in particular, have a tremendous need to have their egos assuaged. A study of mass-movement leaders of the past reveals a distinct pattern: rejection in other fields of endeavor, usually resulting in frustration and self-contempt, which in turn manifest themselves in hatred of others, extreme vanity, and, almost without fail, absolute moralitis. Sounds like a pretty good description of Adolf Hitler, doesn't it?

Because of the mind-set of the group's leader, one has to look carefully beyond the slogans and rituals for his real motives. All too often, the head of a movement feeds his own glory and power at the expense of his followers. If necessary, "needs" can be manufactured in order to keep an organization going. Today, there are probably more self-anointed leaders than ever before who are masters at creating needs. They are able to mask the truth in such a way as to create the perception that their actions are aimed at improving the plight of one group or another.

Above all, most crusade leaders find it easy to be harsh with others, and are usually intolerant and cruel toward those who do not see things their way. In truth, the would-be reformer is a vain individual who is presumptuous enough to believe that everyone should be forced to agree with his views. As Napoleon observed, "Vanity made the revolution; liberty was only a pretext."

When carefully scrutinized, the crusade leader usually turns out to be nothing more than an Absolute Moralist with a banner.

PROFILE OF A HABITUAL JOINER

Without followers, of course, a crusade leader would not get very far. To snare his disciples, he has to compete with every other crusade leader for available bodies, because a joiner . . . is a joiner . . . is a joiner. Although no joiner worth his crusading salt would ever admit it—even to himself—the cause is really secondary to him. To ease the heated competition among recruiters, crusade leaders should agree to hold an annual draft—much like the owners of professional sports teams do—to divvy up each year's crop of talent. As teeny-boppers come of age, they could then be drafted in an orderly fashion by all the crusade leaders who agree to be bound by the draft.

As it now stands, however, champions of various causes have to fight off competitors to make the best possible impression on the pool of prospective joiners. To do so, they employ a variety of motivational techniques for appealing to a wide spectrum of desires and emotional traits. It is essential that a crusade leader understand the would-be follower's motives for joining, which can range from companionship . . . to a desire to conform . . . to ego satisfaction . . . to escape from personal responsibility for his own success and happiness . . . to a genuine belief in the worthiness of the crusade (or at least the belief that he believes).

Following is a discussion of four of the more common motivations for joining a crusade.

BOREDOM

High on the list of motivating factors is boredom. If you are supporting more than one or two (presumably noble) causes, it might be a good idea to recheck your premises. If anyone needs to get a life, it's a professional cause advocate. When the same names and faces keep popping up in conjunction with new causes, it makes one a bit suspicious of what some of these people do for a living. Observing some of the more well-known serial crusaders flitting from one picket line to another, volunteering their comments on why every perceived societal problem is a racial issue and jetting from one country to another to hug communist dictators and terrorists, one cannot help but be curious about who keeps them in new suits, not to mention their air travel and hotel accommodations.

GUILT AND ENVY

Both of these negative emotions play an important role in determining the success of a crusade when it comes to attracting new supporters. Succeed in causing a person to feel guilty enough, or bring to the surface the envy that has long been simmering inside him, and the chances are pretty good that he'll support your cause without engaging in a great deal of due diligence. Guilt and envy are two of the most dangerous motives for joining a cause.

SELF-RIGHTEOUSNESS

Self-righteousness is arrogance at its worst. I concur with Thoreau's view that very few people who claim virtuosity are really deserving of the mantle. We've already been over the problem of others wanting to set moral standards for you, so let me just underscore it with regard to causes. Living a life guided by rational actions requires that you be in control of your mind, beginning with the construction and maintenance of your personal code of ethics.

It goes without saying that just as it is arrogant for anyone to preach morality to you, so, too, is it arrogant for you to preach morality to others—whether directly or under the guise of a cause. It is in your best interest to fight the urge to set moral standards for your fellow man, because not only does such action tend to evolve into aggression, it also takes time away from working on important issues that *are* your business.

IGNORANCE

Lastly, a factor that joiners of all but the most noble of causes have in common is a general ignorance of the facts. Arrogance and ignorance go hand in hand, from whence comes the expression "arrogance of the ignorant." Given how often so-called experts turn out to be wrong in their predictions about the future, one might be justified in concluding that ignorance is almost a necessity for arrogance to exist.

Environmentalists are notorious for this flaw, often hopping from one pet issue to another as new information surfaces that undermines their causes. Though there have been an endless stream of dire predictions about such things as global warming (which, conveniently, took the place of the global-cooling scare that ultimately was annihilated by the facts), depletion of the earth's rain forests (even though the number of trees in the ground actually becomes *greater* every year), and the effects of ozone holes in the atmosphere, the earth seems to go right on spinning, life expectancy rates continue to increase, and the standard of living in industrialized nations continues to climb upward.

In summation, the joiner is a frustrated individual who needs to be needed to an excessive degree. Self-contempt is a common trademark among joiners, which makes it easy for the joiner to lockstep with his leader in expressing contempt for others. Previous failures drive him to remove the burden of personal responsibility from his own shoulders, which he believes he can accomplish by becoming lost in the group. When he becomes a faceless body in a common cause, the pressure for personal success is lifted and he is ripe to become a full-fledged Absolute Moralist. The promised glory of the future is precisely what takes his mind off his current misery. The group becomes a sort of narcotic for him by lessening his pain.

The professional crusader also finds it safer to vent his feelings of hostility under the banner of a group. When lost in the faceless depths of a movement, it is not he, but the group, that is interfering in the lives of others. Because of his own perceived sacrifices, cruelty and hatred toward others become justifiable. Crusades are a source of perverse freedom—the freedom to be harsh and intolerant toward others, the freedom to pressure those who are perceived to be enemies, and the freedom to interfere in people's lives without feeling guilty about it.

The pathological joiner must also possess the ability to ignore all rational arguments that threaten to undermine "the cause." This ostrich-like mind-set gives the joiner the strength to confront the obstacles and contradictions that constantly arise. By his refusal to see or hear anything that does not fit in with the crusade's narrative, such obstacles and contradictions simply fail to exist. It is understandable, then, that the most successful crusades have been those that are most effective at keeping their followers separated from reality.

Because crusades have so much in common, the chronic joiner finds it easy to jump from one cause to another. After all, if the basic characteristics of most crusades are indistinguishable and the traits of their members similar, crusade hopping is easy to justify. You may be acquainted with someone who is group addicted. If

so, ask yourself how many times that person has embraced a new cause and each time proclaimed, in effect, that *this* cause is different than all of the other causes he has previously supported.

An easy way to check yourself against vulnerability to the Crusade Hurdle is to examine the number of times you have jumped on new causes, as well as how fast and how radically you have made such jumps. Habitual joiners tend to jump often, quickly, and radically, because they are victims of the **Confused-Thinking Theory**, which states: *When a person's philosophy takes a sudden and dramatic shift in direction, his reasoning is suspect, because:*

1. *If his previous beliefs were foreign to his present viewpoints, his original thinking must have been flawed. If so, how can he trust his reasoning power with regard to his current beliefs?*

2. *If his original thinking was sound, his past beliefs should have been correct. If so, his reasons for joining the new crusade must be flawed.*

While the outward characteristics of all movements are similar, the nature of their stated objectives can be quite different. If you're in the habit of making radical swings in your basic beliefs, the Crusade Hurdle is still in your path. But if you're on the looking-out-for-number-one track, the evolution of your belief system should continue in the same general direction. Carefully monitor your thoughts whenever you stumble onto a new group or movement that stirs your emotions, *especially* if its cause seems to be the answer to all of the world's perceived ills.

A RATIONAL VIEW OF CRUSADES

Two of the more important keys to getting a person to join a crusade is a lack of knowledge and/or rational thought. If everyone who joined a movement, cause, or crusade carefully analyzed the realities of the group's purpose in advance, I strongly suspect that most crusades throughout history would have disappeared without a whimper for lack of membership.

There are many reasons why group action is irrational from the individual's standpoint, and perhaps the most important one is that the group may never accomplish its intended purpose. In which case the joiner is apt to become bitter about the time and energy he has wasted, time and energy that could have been used to better his own life.

In part, this explains why so many hard-core followers of crusades come from the Diaper Corps. Once an individual has some real-world experience under his belt, he is far more experienced in the workings of life and thus far more hesitant to waste his finite supply of time on a cause that others happen to believe is worthy.

In many respects, there is not strength in numbers, but weakness. Suppose you want to help "the poor." Charity is a noble activity, assuming you can afford the time and/or money to engage in it. If it makes you feel good to help those who are less fortunate than you, by all means do so. But rather than waste time becoming involved in the muddled bureaucracy of some organization where you would have to confer with others over such questions as who qualifies as "poor" and what, precisely, should be done for such people, would it not be easier, faster, and more efficient to make all necessary decisions unilaterally and take immediate action yourself?

All you would need to do is decide which person or persons *you* deem to be poor, then decide how much of *your* money you would like them to have. Best of all, you could personally deliver the money to them—no middleman. Just think, you could do all this without having to stop and consult with anyone else. Having accomplished your purpose, you could then go on to other pursuits without harassing friends, neighbors, or strangers about your beliefs. Simple, efficient, immediate results—the kind of results that are all but impossible to achieve through group action.

If you acted in precisely the above manner, I would be inclined to believe you if you told me you had a desire to help the poor. But if you tried to solicit me to join a charitable organization to help those who are in financial need, I would look you over real carefully and ask a whole bunch of questions that you probably either couldn't answer or would prefer not to.

Since it's very easy to help others if that is your true purpose, I'm skeptical of the motives of do-gooders who form organizations to carry out charitable and "public good" projects. The first thing I look for in such people is a big ego; second, I look for an ulterior motive behind their purported intent.

The next time you're tempted to work for a charity, or even contribute to one, I suggest you ask yourself the following questions: Do I have firsthand knowledge of exactly how the money I am raising is going to be spent? Can I be certain it is being used to help those the group purports to be aiding? And, if so, do I really know what percentage of the money, after bureaucratic waste, will actually end up in the hands of the designated recipients? People who gave to charities targeted to help impoverished Haitians after that country's catastrophic earthquake in 2010 have been dismayed to discover that almost nothing has been done to help those most ravaged by the quake.

Even if a crusade is successful (and keeping in mind that *successful* is a subjective term), you have no way of knowing that you will live long enough to witness the results. To work on a crusade all your life and not be around to see its fruition would be a cruel fate indeed. From this perspective, the crusade's emphasis on the future can be seen for the sham it really is.

This, I believe, is the key that holds the Islamic death-and-destruction movement together. The stated mission of this hate crusade is to eliminate from the face of the earth every "infidel." Since this objective can never be accomplished, there is no pressure for a final result from mindless followers. Which is why you can count on the radical Islamic movement to go on in perpetuity. As to rewards, radical Islam is perhaps the perfect crusade, because martyrs are led to believe that their return on time invested comes in the afterlife—which means there is no danger of their ever being able to convey to other followers the reality that things didn't work out quite the way they expected.

But there is an even worse fate possible: What if the group's stated purpose *is* accomplished during your lifetime, but the results turn out to be very different from what you had in mind all those years that you were donating your valuable time-and-energy resources to help bring them about? Although most groups never come close to achieving their stated objectives, disillusionment is the rule rather than the exception for those that do.

The reason for this is obvious. Given that each person in an organization is unique, your perception of the group's purpose and the perception of the group's leader—not to mention the perception of every other member of the group—are likely to be quite different. You can be certain that the masses in the early years of the Bolshevik Revolution in Russia were not envisioning the same results as the leaders who proclaimed that communism would free them. As in George Orwell's *1984*, they had no idea that the freedom promised by the Bolshevik leaders would translate into slavery. Ditto with Castro's Cuba, Mao's China, and Ho Chi Minh's Vietnam.

Finally, the hardest reality of all for the Diaper Corps to grasp: Your own personal growth in knowledge and reasoning power may shed a whole new light on a cause you once thought to be worthwhile. New facts continually arise that may take the glitter off a once seemingly worthy crusade. The great author and futurist Alvin Toffler (*Future Shock*, *The Third Wave*, *Power Shift*) wrote that when he was a Marxist in his late teens and early twenties, he, "like many young people, thought [he] had all the answers." He went on to write, "I soon learned that my 'answers' were partial, one-sided, and obsolete."

Thus, in most cases, joining a crusade is hard to justify. If you join a crusade just to conform, you are not acting rationally. If you join for companionship, you are being dishonest with the other members of the group (unless that is the group's stated purpose). If you join for ego satisfaction, you're on dangerous ground, because the more you feed your ego, the hungrier it gets—which only leads you further from a rational course of action. And if you join out of frustration, you're taking the easy way out in order to avoid real solutions to your problems—not to mention inviting additional frustration into your life as a result of not being able to get others to see things your way.

THE EFFICIENCY OF INDIVIDUAL ACTION

Perhaps the most critical element that professional cause advocates fail to factor into their crusade equations is technological advance. Not only does technology continually render perceived crises irrelevant, it also continues to raise the living standards of potential cause joiners. In our modern age of prosperity, nothing annoys crusade leaders more than the realization that otherwise perfectly good prospects for their causes are relaxing in the backyards of their suburban homes, grilling steaks on the barbecue, and watching their kids splash around in their ten-by-twenty-foot swimming pools. Convincing these folks that they're being exploited by "the rich" is a pretty tough sell.

Even if you believed in a group's objectives and actually had firsthand knowledge of the facts, it still would be less complicated and more efficient to act on your own rather than in concert with others. In addition, as previously pointed out, collective action encourages one to avoid personal responsibility.

As with the charity example discussed earlier, if you feel strongly about a cause, by acting alone you can start doing something about it immediately. But if your approach is to build a sophisticated organizational structure to promote the cause, you may never get around to your stated purpose. The nature of such organizational efforts—endless politics, debates over differences of opinion, funding, and other bureaucratic obstacles—can easily use up all your available time and energy. All too often, the organizational effort becomes an end in itself.

If you feel a sincere urge to take action for or against something, don't waste time trying to convert others to your way of thinking. If you believe in a particular philosophy, you should be too busy living it to spend time trying to convert others to your way of thinking. If you have a desire to have your ideas heard, why not write a book about them or offer to lecture on those ideas for a fee?

Above all, don't feel that you have a moral obligation to help people "see the light." Chances are pretty good that you have enough problems of your own that require your full time and attention. Life burdens us with too many nonproductive projects as it is—from brushing our teeth to getting our hair cut to filling our gas tanks—so why look for more? The fact is that the world doesn't have problems; people have problems.

Notwithstanding all the real or imagined world-disaster crises, the reality is that you have it within your power to lead a fulfilling, meaningful life—starting *right now*. Perceived disasters that may or may not make their appearance in your lifetime—or ever—should not be allowed to rob you of that opportunity, nor should those who choose to spend their time crusading to save the world from such perceived disasters.

Looking out for number one requires that you maintain control over your actions rather than allowing the desires of a group to determine them for you. Unfortunately, millions of individuals have to spend a significant amount of their valuable time and energy fending off those who constantly try to interfere in their lives through crusades. Don't allow yourself to be emotionally swept along by the herd instinct, the rhetoric of Absolute Moralists, or the slogans of a mindless band of people. Staunchly refuse to yield to the intimidating pressures of others to become involved in group action.

A group may dwell endlessly on how it can help you become a happier individual, but such claims are meaningless. Why? Because the very premise of group action negates that possibility. When you contribute time and subordinate your interests to those of an organization, you lose not only your individuality, but also precious, irreplaceable hours that could be spent confronting obstacles in your own life.

To a rational individual, the farther off the promised results, the more obvious it is that perpetuation of the group itself is the real objective of the leader. So when the next crusader comes knocking at your door, babbling about this or that crisis, do yourself a favor and advise him to get a real job, get out of the way of those who are creating value for others, and allow entrepreneurial creativity to continue expanding the frontiers of modern technology and improving the living standards of people worldwide.

Using your time and energy to help promote a cause that advocates the use of force to make others accept an agenda that certain individuals believe is right is far removed from the noble objective of having a legitimate purpose in life, being passionate about that purpose, and taking continual and constructive action to achieve it. If you wish to make a serious contribution to world peace and prosperity, I suggest you use your time and energy to improve the one person over which you not only have control, but the moral authority to control: *you.*

If you do decide to become involved in a crusade, just make certain that you do so for rational reasons—*your* rational reasons. And be doubly certain that you are honest with yourself about your motives. Any rational motive is fine, so long as you understand exactly what you're doing and why you're doing it.

Also, be careful not to chastise others for not becoming involved in a cause that you believe to be worthy. How others spend their time and what they believe in is none of your business. When you start being so presumptuous as to concern yourself with getting others to become involved in a cause you believe in, you are taking the first step toward becoming a crusader.

On the other hand, if you make the decision to focus on your own life rather than becoming involved in a crusade in an attempt to solve some group's perception of a societal problem, I wish to extend my personal thanks to you for eliminating yourself as a burden to the rest of mankind—as well as my congratulations for your success in clearing the Crusade Hurdle.

5 The Financial Hurdle

There are those who protest that making money shouldn't be so important, that there are other things in life that are far more rewarding than financial success. And I happen to agree with them. Nevertheless, numerous polls have found that poor people—regardless of their country of residence—tend to be unhappy. Such polls clearly show that the vast majority of people on this planet care a great deal about money, *especially* those who have very little of it.

Though you may not be on the verge of starvation, the odds are pretty good that you're struggling to maintain your present living standard. Expenses have a way of increasing in direct proportion to rising income, the result being that most people never achieve financial peace of mind.

Money, of course, is really just a means to an end. But, paradoxically, if your mind is cluttered with thoughts of financial instability, it tends to blind you to the reality that the best things in life are free. In today's tension-filled, materialistic world, it's unrealistic for the average person to hold out hopes for clear-minded happiness without achieving a reasonable degree of financial stability.

Perhaps the most important commodity money can buy is freedom. I'm not so naïve as to believe that money can buy total freedom, because so long as governments exist, absolute freedom is beyond reach. Nonetheless, you are likely to have much more freedom *with* money than without it. Just having peace of mind is a great liberation in itself. Being free to think pleasant thoughts instead of stewing over financial problems is not a freedom to be taken lightly.

Clearing the Financial Hurdle means having the freedom to act out of self-choice rather than basing your actions on chance or the choice of others. Only you can be the judge of how much financial success it would take to achieve the freedom you desire. For one person it might mean making $75,000 a year, while for another person it could mean an annual income of $500,000. How much it takes to achieve the kind of freedom that allows you to feel in control of your life is up to you. It's *your* life, so don't allow anyone else to make that decision for you.

When it comes to making money, it's important to guard against setting yourself up for disillusionment. If you've managed to achieve financial success, you already know that it doesn't buy happiness. People who dream about the day when money will no longer be a problem often expect something from financial success that it cannot deliver.

I was guilty of that mistake the first time I made a lot of money. Instead of the nirvana I had envisioned, what I found was the real world all over again, just on a higher financial level. I became disillusioned and tried to compensate in other ways, but that only made things worse. At the time, I didn't realize that what I was really after was happiness and that money was just a means to achieving that end.

As I matured, I came to realize that the pot at the end of the financial rainbow was actually filled with freedom. I also recognized that time was the limiting factor in the financial equation, so it was not good enough just to work toward the day when I would have enough money to obtain the freedom I sought. As much happiness as possible had to be achieved while making the climb. The day I mentally transformed the climb itself from a struggle to a joy was a major turning point in my life.

If you lose sight of the reality that money represents a means to an end, you risk getting caught up in the self-perpetual success cycle, i.e., the more financial success you achieve, the more success you desire. Of and by itself, this is not necessarily a bad thing. The problem, however, is that people who get caught up in the self-perpetual success cycle usually fail to take the time to think about what it is they really want out of life. At its extreme, it can become a form of self-imprisonment.

Buddha explained it insightfully when he said, "Excessive desire makes us slaves of whatever we crave. Everyone has seen this principle in operation—a craving for food, a craving for popularity, a craving for success. All make us lose our freedom to choose wisely."

So, while making money is important, you should strive to keep wealth and material possessions in proper perspective. The most appealing aspect of financial success is that it can rid you of many of your day-to-day burdens, burdens that can sap your limited supply of time and energy. In turn, ridding yourself of those burdens frees you to concentrate on the things that matter most to you.

A MELANCHOLY STROLL DOWN LOSER'S LANE

If you've never experienced the misery of failure, the chances are pretty good that you haven't tried very hard to succeed. I've never met anyone who has made it to the top—and managed to stay there—who didn't first taste the bitterness of defeat, usually many defeats.

Failure, in fact, is a good indicator of both the effort you've expended and your willingness to pay the price of financial success. Disraeli cut to the chase with his simple observation, "There's no education like adversity." I've acquired a good deal of knowledge from my successes, but not nearly as much as I have from my failures. In fact, I would go so far as to say that virtually every setback I've experienced has turned out to be a long-term blessing in disguise. Even more important than knowledge, I believe one gains far more wisdom from failure than from success. One danger of success is that it can lead one to ignorantly believe he is infallible. Following is a painful personal story that underscores this point. The result was a considerable amount of short-term suffering but an abundance of long-term wisdom that led to great long-term success.

After dabbling in the record and film industries for a short period of time, as well as a number of other entrepreneurial hallucinations intended to fatten the ego and slim the wallet, I awoke one morning to find myself facing the following quadrangle of financial facts: (1) an overhead of about $30,000 a month; (2) no income; (3) a bank balance of $11.37; and (4) debts of about $500,000.

I remember lying back on a chaise lounge next to my swimming pool and allowing my mind to drift nostalgically as I gazed out over the estate of my next-door neighbor, movie mogul Jack Warner. Since I had the only second-floor swimming pool in Beverly Hills, I had the advantage of being able to enjoy a view of Warner's massive grounds—private golf course and all—while sitting around my pool.

By finally setting aside the *ought to's* of my situation and facing up to the *is's*, I arrived at the astonishing conclusion that I had a serious problem. (Duh!) Reality was starting to set in. As is always the case, reality had remained stubbornly incontrovertible and had simply ignored my desires, false perceptions, and outrageous lifestyle.

As I departed the patio and walked through my bedroom, my mind drifted back to the pitch the realtor had given me the first time I had looked at my palatial residence. It was all very exciting then—the stories about Marilyn Monroe having once lived there and how Mickey Rooney used to dive out the master-bedroom window into the second-story swimming pool at those wild, long-ago Hollywood parties.

Exciting, yes—but insane. At the time I concluded the deal, nature must have been smiling over my shoulder and saying, "Boy, am I ever going to stick it to you. Nobody violates my laws and gets away with it." To express it in the simplest of clichés, once I moved into the house, the game was over. One by one, my three Mercedes and my Cadillac were repossessed. I was down to living in a mansion, with no wheels to take me anywhere.

Can you imagine living in Los Angeles without a car? I couldn't even afford groceries. I was getting panicky, to the point of eyeing the cat food in the pantry. I started selling off what was left of my furniture, but the money was quickly swallowed up by alert creditors who were stalking me around the clock. The phones were disconnected and my gas and electric were ready to go any day.

What to do? Where to go? Finally, time ran out. I didn't know that when sheriff's deputies come to hand you your walking papers, they arrive in pairs. When I opened the door, I was staring at two shiny law-enforcement badges pinned to two gigantic chests. I gave the law-enforcement ghouls a warm hello, then threw out a couple of one-liners in a feeble attempt to make pleasant small talk. No smiles . . . only cold stares.

The dynamic duo handed me my walking papers, matter-of-factly spewed out some memorized legalese, then departed. The only thing they made perfectly clear was that they would be back in five days to check the premises, and if they were to find a tortoise inside, he could expect to be unceremoniously booted out on his shell. I believed them. I always believe people who wear guns on their belts.

By selling some of my furniture for about ten cents on the dollar, I managed to scrape together enough money to rent a truck. For the next five days, I was in a stupor, walking back and

"(Gulp!) Have you guys heard the one about . . ."

forth through the institutional-length hallways of my magnificent home, going up and down the winding staircase, climbing into the back of the truck to load my belongings, and trying to organize my worldly possessions inside the eighteen-foot van.

After a while, all I wanted to do was sleep, but I was down to just forty-eight hours . . . then thirty-six . . . then, finally, only twenty-four hours remained until my uniformed friends were scheduled to be back on my doorstep searching for reptiles. Every so often I would wake up on the floor, in the middle of a room, anxiously glance at my watch and realize, to my horror, that I had inadvertently fallen asleep for an hour or two. I was running out of time!

I never did get all of my possessions out of the house. When E-Day (i.e., Eviction Day) arrived, I was forced to leave thousands of dollars' worth of clothes and other personal belongings behind. I can vividly recall my final trip down the stairs, loaded down with personal belongings. I departed through the back of the house to get one final look at the patio, the pool, and the view of the lavish grounds Jack Warner had so generously, albeit unknowingly, shared with me. As I looked out over the incredible beauty of it all for the last time—hangers of clothes draped over my back—two thoughts went through my mind, thoughts that would prove to be my salvation in the long struggle ahead.

First, I harbored no malice toward anyone—not my creditors, not the government henchmen who were due to arrive at my door at any moment, not anyone else who had contributed to my pain. I did, however, harbor a great disdain for *myself.* What a fool I had been. I had violated every principle I had worked so hard to discover and nurture, principles that had consistently produced positive results for me when I religiously adhered to them. I had chosen to ignore the certainty that sooner or later nature would hand me a bill for my irresponsible actions. Now, the time had arrived, and nature was presenting me with a tab so enormous that there appeared to be no way out.

Second, I said to myself, "I'll be back, bigger and better than ever. I'll pay the price, whatever it is, but I'll be back." With that, I descended the stairs for the last time, threw the final load of my belongings into the rear of the truck, climbed behind the wheel, and pulled away. As I chugged down the street, I couldn't help thinking of the contrast between the truck I was driving and the majestic homes, manicured lawns, and beautiful palm trees that surrounded me. And the contrast was magnified when the sheriff's car passed me no more than a half block from my house, going in the other direction. As certified government sadists, they undoubtedly were disappointed to find that the old homestead had been abandoned. Marilyn Monroe was dead; Mickey Rooney hadn't been in the pool for years; and The Tortoise had moved to his new home: a Ryder truck.

LEPROSY IN BEVERLY HILLS

When you go broke in Omaha or Des Moines or Memphis, you make for good cocktail-party stories. Of course, most of your old acquaintances would just as soon not be seen with you, and you get the usual blackball treatment everywhere you go. But at least there's no spitting. Not so in Beverly Hills. In the Golden Ghetto, they actually spit on you.

Heaven forbid you should go broke in Beverly Hills, where bankruptcy is synonymous with leprosy. No one even talks about you at cocktail parties. You're yesterday's news; you're dead. If you'd just stay off the streets, the beautiful people would be happy to leave you alone. Just don't become an eyesore, or all of those clueless Hollywood liberals who drone on endlessly about the plight of the homeless will have you arrested.

Don't get me wrong. Beverly Hills has nothing against diseases. The residents just don't like lepers cluttering up the view of their swank shops and chic boutiques. The degradation and humiliation are impossible for me to adequately describe, so let it just suffice to say that Loser's Lane in Beverly Hills is the loneliest, most humbling, most demeaning street on the face of the planet.

Like so many things in life that are healthy for you in the long term, suffering is not something you would choose if you could avoid it. Nonetheless, it's stimulating, because it forces you to be self-analytical and use your wits on the obstacles you face. I recall a prominent entertainer friend of mine consoling me by saying that he, too, had once fallen into the financial abyss, and assuring me that the trip down is precisely what brings forth a person's greatest creativity. That, he said, is the source of the soul power that so many music greats possess.

As it turned out, he was absolutely right, because I am convinced, from a long-term point of view, that it was the best thing that ever happened to me. When you're at the bottom, you have two choices: You either roll over and die or you fight back. The one certainty is that you will never solve your problems by running from them.

Or watch the things you gave your life to, broken,
And stoop and build 'em up with worn-out tools.

As creditors scoured the bushes looking for me, things began to heat up. What stands out most in my memory is the sadistic enthusiasm of so many of the creditors and collection agents who were on the hunt for The Tortoise. For some of them, it became akin to a crusade. When you're the one being chased, your perception is that you are the focal point of every collection agent's life.

Every now and then, Legalman (commonly referred to by laymen as "attorney" or "lawyer") succeeded in serving me with papers, which usually led to a default judgment. But that was only a dead end for him. Whether a deposition was being taken or a default judgment being entered, Legalman, much to his dismay, was forced to face the frustrating reality that the bare bones of a financial corpse could not be converted into dollars at his command. As a result, his sadistic zeal usually turned to bewilderment rather quickly. To give you an idea of Legalman's frustration, I quote verbatim from the transcript of one such deposition:

Legalman: "Where do you now live?"

The Tortoise: "Right now, I'm living on a truck."

Legalman: "Could you be a little more specific about that?"

The Tortoise: "It's a Ryder truck—R-y-d-e-r."

Legalman: "Who owns the truck?"

The Tortoise: "The Ryder Company, I guess. I leased it from them."

Legalman: "When did you do that?"

The Tortoise: "When the sheriff put me out of my house."

If it was possible to experience joy in the midst of financial devastation, it might have been at that moment, watching Legalman scratch his head, peep over the rims of his glasses, and display a totally perplexed look in front of his client.

Notwithstanding the grim realities, it became clear that Legalman honestly believed I had devised some sinister plan to secretly stash away untold piles of cash. Unfortunately for both him and me, such was not the case. The ghastly truth was that the cupboards really were bare. And when the aroma of money is absent, Legalman quickly loses interest. His grab-the-chips-and-run approach to practicing law was a great aid to me in keeping the harassment down to near-humane levels during many delicate moments over the next couple of years.

THE ROAD TO FREEDOM

The purpose of describing my lowest ebb was to give you a better perspective of your own financial situation. You may just be getting out of college; you may be someone pushing forty and working ten to twelve hours a day at a job you don't enjoy; you may be a woman who's had it with being a slave to her house and family, longing to get into the work force; or you may be an executive with a high income and all the material comforts of life, but no time to enjoy them.

Whatever your present situation, if you're not free, if you're not able to spend the majority of your time on activities and pursuits that make life worth living, there is a way out. There's a way to get from where you are now to where you want to be. I did it from the most impossible set of circumstances imaginable; many others have done it; and you can do it if you want it badly enough.

Whether you're facing the standard variety of poverty or suburban poverty (high income offset by equally high overhead), the same formula applies. And the first step in the formula I'm referring to is to convince yourself that you can wipe the slate clean and start over again in another direction. Until you understand and believe this truth, you are not ready to take the kind of action needed to improve the quality of your life.

Always keep in mind that there's a big difference between *difficult* and *impossible*. No one can force you to take the easy way out. Al Pacino eloquently made this point in his Oscar-winning role in *Scent of a Woman*. Said Pacino's character, retired Lieutenant Colonel Frank Slade, "I always knew what the right path was. Without exception, I knew. But I never took it. You know why? It was too damn hard." Translation: You *always* have a choice, but most people are not willing to pay the price.

If your Weight-and-Balance Happiness Scale is receiving sound data from you, it will present you with rational answers; i.e., answers that are in your long-term best interest. When your scale is functioning properly, it will remind you that you have only one life to live and that it makes no sense to waste that one precious life doing things you don't enjoy. And, in the final analysis, it will tell you that *you* are the only one who possesses the power to hold you back. No one else can prevent you from going after what you want out of life. Finally, your scale should repeatedly spell out the price you'll need to pay for a better life so you can make an intelligent decision as to whether or not the price is worth it.

Keeping in mind the reality of relativity, I find it psychologically healthy to look at financial success as a game. Games are fun to win, but no matter how many chips you accumulate, the reality is that all you'll be taking with you when the game ends is a quart of embalming fluid.

Next, don't waste time sitting around and daydreaming about the way you wish things would be. Instead, acknowledge how they really are, then focus on ways to turn those realities into opportunities. Make an honest evaluation of your present circumstances and ask yourself if you're satisfied with your lot in life. If the answer is affirmative, then stay put, stop complaining, and enjoy yourself.

But if you don't feel good about where you are financially, it's up to you to make a commitment to change things—whether it's your job, your profession, or your business. The one thing you do not want to do is spend the rest of your life drowning in regret. Continually remind yourself that change is hard but not impossible. Looking out for number one requires conscious, rational decisions, and it's simply not rational to spend the rest of your life being disappointed and unhappy.

THE SOLUTION IN THE MIRROR

I again emphasize that one of my final thoughts as I departed my Beverly Hills mansion was that I was mad at no one but myself. This mind-set was my saving grace. It was I who had sabotaged The Tortoise. It was I who had made the decisions that led to my downfall. It was I, and I alone, who was responsible for my dilemma.

Being bitter at others who contributed to your problems is not only a waste of time and energy, it's a bore to everyone around you. Never forget that the same guy whom you think shafted you in a business deal probably has a hundred reasons for believing he was justified in doing whatever he did. Everyone sees the world through his own biased perspective.

Before I made it up the financial ladder the first time around, I conditioned myself to be grateful to those lecherous souls who pilfered my chips, because they gave me the opportunity to learn through my mistakes. I worked hard at radiating my hostilities inward—where they belonged. I took the position that it was up to me to protect my chips, and if became lax I deserved to suffer the consequences.

Never waste valuable time and energy being mad at the person whom you believe caused your downfall. In the final analysis, it was you who made your decisions, and one of the unfortunate decisions you may have made was to become involved with the wrong person. It's healthy to think of the guy who separated you from your chips as merely a vehicle you used to punish yourself. Fortunately, in the final analysis, universal laws prevail, and you will end up exactly where you deserve to be. And so, too, will the other person. So do yourself a favor and forget about the injustice someone may have done to you, and instead focus on the mistakes *you* made.

I can assure you that I spent a lot of time on that Ryder truck browbeating myself to the point where I was appalled by my own ignorance and carelessness. As a result, my desire to succeed went beyond just making money. Rehabilitating my self-respect became a burning desire for me.

The same principle applies to being bitter at friends for "letting you down" during tough times. Such a misdirected focus avoids the real issue. Sure, plenty of people forgot who I was when I went down in flames, but that's life. To forgive isn't divine, it's rational. I came to this conclusion through the following analysis:

- Being bitter toward someone else had no relevance whatsoever to solving my financial problems, and thus did not warrant an expenditure of my time or energy.

- Since my friends and acquaintances were human beings, they were subject to human weaknesses, and it's a natural instinct for humans, as well as rats, to abandon sinking ships.

- My friends had nothing whatsoever to do with my financial problems, so why should they be involved in my misery?

- Since friendships, like everything else in life, should be based on mutual value, I concluded that I must not have contributed much value to those relationships that did not survive my downfall. The only other explanation was that I was guilty of making bad friendship choices in the first place. But, in either case, it was clear to me that it was I who had some adjustments to make.

- Finally, whenever anyone shut me out of his life, I figured it was his way of telling me that he didn't have confidence in my ability to make it back. And if that was the case, I lost confidence in *his* ability to make sound judgments, because I was *certain* I was going to make it back. I therefore viewed it as the other person's loss, because he had voluntarily removed himself from my life by displaying poor judgment in sizing up my character, my mental toughness, and my abilities.

When things go bad, it's imperative that you keep your eye on the ball and continue moving toward solutions to your problems. If others make mistakes in judging you, that's their problem—and not an uncommon problem, at that. People make mistakes every day.

While turning your anger inward is healthy, being mad at the world is a waste of time. It will do absolutely nothing for your cause to sit around and be bitter. If you are now making this error, I urge you to revise your mind-set as quickly as possible. Whether you are sixteen or sixty, every day spent being bitter about what others may have done to you is one more day subtracted from your limited, dwindling supply of time on this earth.

Excuses

A surefire formula for failure is to concentrate on excuses rather than positive action. Nothing is as easy to dwell on as an excuse, and nothing complicates life more easily. An excuse may be justifiable, but the reality is that it will do nothing whatsoever to improve your life. An excuse focuses on the past; a solution focuses on the present and future.

A favorite standby, of course, is the so-called bad break. Is there such a thing as a bad break? Yes, and everyone has more than his share. Old Man Murphy doesn't play favorites. He does a pretty good job of meting out obstacles on a fairly equal basis.

The difference lies in the manner in which each of us handles misfortune.

People who use bad breaks as excuses are often victims of the **World-Owes-Me-a-Living Theory**, which states: *Anyone who believes that others—or, worse, "the world"—owes them something are destined for failure and disappointment.* Until a person cleanses this poisonous notion from his mind, he is unlikely to leave the starting gate, much less win the race.

Labeling oneself is among the most popular ways to avoid personal responsibility in our modern-day culture of whiners and complainers. It's a convenient ploy, but one that is not supported by reality, so never allow yourself to get lulled into the labeling trap. In this regard, the "glass ceiling" and "double-standard pay scale" are two favorites of women's rights groups, but a woman focused on creating value doesn't have time to get bogged down in such issues. By attaching herself to "women's causes," she underrates her own unique abilities.

Today, the number of women in major roles in both industry and government is undeniable. Did the glass ceiling stop Oprah? Or ABC's Diane Sawyer or Robin Roberts? Or Condoleezza Rice? Or any of the hundreds of women who hold upper echelon positions such as chairman, president, and CEO of major corporations?

Some might be inclined to say, "That's all right for a handful of women who have exceptional talent, but what about the rest of us?" To that question I would respond that your focus should not be on others. It's not a question of whether you have more or less ability than someone else. It's a matter of discovering what *your* unique abilities are, then exploiting those abilities to their fullest extent. The same principles apply on every level of the financial ladder.

Take, for example, laws that force restaurant owners not to discriminate when it comes to hiring. This can result in white waiters working in a soul-food restaurant or black waiters working in a Chinese restaurant. What's wrong with this? Plenty. From both a constitutional and Natural Law standpoint, no one has a right to force a business owner to hire *anyone*. The restaurant is *his* asset, and an individual has a natural right to do whatever he wishes with his own property, including "discriminating" to his heart's content.

Some people argue that the government has an inherent duty to enforce its will in "public places," and a restaurant is often used as an example of a public place. But the reality is that a restaurant is *not* a public place; it is a privately owned enterprise. If an owner chooses to not hire Latinos, men, women, blacks, or whites, and I don't approve of his hiring policies, I can take immediate steps to do something about it—*on my own*—by simply not frequenting his business.

The above example is what free enterprise is all about. If Absolute Moralists would just leave it alone, it would work fine, automatically adjusting itself to meet consumer demands. When an owner sets a rule regarding his own retail establishment, and that rule is too widely rejected, the workings of the free-enterprise system will respond by forcing him out of business. He doesn't need an unconstitutional law to go broke; he can do that quite easily on his own.

What I'm getting at here is that you should never lower yourself to fight for the "right" to be where you are not wanted. It's a mistake to look to government force or any other type of coercion to help you clear the Financial Hurdle. While it may get you what you want in the short term, force does not work over the long term. You will never fully exploit your skills if you work in an atmosphere of resentment.

Irrespective of what left-wing intellectuals would like us to believe, there is an abundant supply of employers whose rational self-interest motivates them to hire the best available talent—without regard to race or sex. In fact, no capitalist who practices rational self-interest would think of doing otherwise. The more competitors make the self-destructive mistake of prejudicial hiring practices, the better it is for those who do not. It's a matter of self-interest.

Being black, female, elderly, or handicapped is just one fact about you, and, in most cases, not relevant with regard to your ability to perform your job. Even if you play the victim role to the hilt and manage to convince others that it's the primary deterrent to your success, it still will not pay your rent. It's a much better idea to focus on convincing a prospective employer that he should hire you for one reason and one reason only: *because you can offer him more value than anyone else.*

PREREQUISITES

After all excuses have been set aside, the first question to ask yourself is what you really want to do with your life, and, in that regard, there are two factors you should take into consideration. One is how you can most effectively use your unique talents to get what you want. The second is to choose a line of work that you genuinely enjoy.

Fortunately, these two factors complement one another. If you do something you enjoy, the odds are that it's also the thing that will give you the best and quickest results. Which is why *you* have to be the judge. Only you know what makes you happy. Two critical rules to follow when making this decision are:

1. Never pursue a career just because someone else wants you to. The person who advises you—whether it be your mother, your wife, or a well-meaning friend—will not have to endure the frustration and dissatisfaction that result from working at something you don't enjoy. Do not make the mistake of trying to be what someone else thinks you should be.

2. Never listen to anyone who tries to convince you that what you are contemplating is too unrealistic or too hard, or that it's too late for you to undertake it. If it's what you've always wanted to do, *do it*. Keep in mind the old stock-market axiom about the public always being wrong. Take a cue from Jonathan Livingston Seagull and don't be afraid to spread your wings above the negative masses.

NATURE'S OMNIPRESENT REALITY: PRICE-PAYING

Price-paying can be a dreary activity, so much so that after a while you might begin to wonder why it doesn't just go away and leave you alone. Unfortunately, it won't. Whether you like it or not, the Price-Paying Toll Machine will always stand between you and your goals. And the annoying thing about this machine is that it never malfunctions. You either pay the required toll or it doesn't let you pass. There are no exceptions.

So, after carefully deciding what you really want to do with your life, the next step is to face up to the cost. Don't kid yourself and try to imagine that you're going to get off easy. The price that will be required of you will depend on a number of factors, such as the importance of your non-financial objectives, your emotional makeup, your skills, and who the most important people in your life are.

Such factors as these, coupled with the extent of your financial aspirations, will determine the price you can expect to pay in terms of time, energy, money, and the jealousy and the resentment of others, not to mention having less time with friends and family and the sacrifice of countless other activities that may now be an important part of your life. This is where you need to do some really serious factual meditation (i.e., thinking about the facts of your situation in a relaxed environment). You should analyze the total price, on your own, without input from others. If your Weight-and-Balance Happiness Scale is functioning properly—which is dependent upon your feeding it correct information—it should be able to determine whether the price you will have to pay is worth what you hope to gain in return.

REASSESS YOUR BAGGAGE

In Chapter 2, I discussed the importance of ridding yourself of excess baggage. If you allow too many unnecessary burdens to enter, and remain, in your life, you'll end up fighting the predators in the Money Game with one arm tied behind your back.

For example, if you're trying to support someone in luxury when your financial situation isn't up to the task, you're playing in quicksand. Or if you're married to or living with a person who isn't patient and understanding—who is not sympathetic to your goals—it's tantamount to having a traitor in your ranks. A nonsupportive domestic partner can sap you of valuable time and energy. If you're in love with someone who fits either of these descriptions, you may be faced with one of the biggest price-paying decisions you'll ever have to make: Is your desire for financial success strong enough to part ways with your mate?

If you're like most people, you probably have a great many burdens in your life, and it's crucial to your financial success that you rid yourself of as many of those burdens as possible. If you're serious about clearing the Financial Hurdle, you simply can't afford the extra baggage.

The Heaviest Bag of All

The heaviest of all excess baggage is an inflated ego, particularly if it controls you rather than the other way around. Everyone has an ego, so don't delude yourself into believing you don't. It's far better to acknowledge the existence of your ego and consciously work to keep it under control. Most people can't afford the price of both an overstuffed ego and financial success. In fact, the cost of such an ego often *is* the foregoing of financial success.

A mega-ego is like a dinosaur lying on your front lawn. If you don't continually feed it, it might just decide get up and step on your house. At its extreme, a bloated ego can result in egoruptcy, a form of bankruptcy caused by the investment of too much time and capital in vanity. Avoid business dealings with anyone afflicted with egoruptcy, because when he goes down for the final count, he's liable to take you with him. Feeding the ego is habit-forming and can lead the addict to commit dishonest acts in his desperation to feed his habit.

Following are some telltale signs that an individual is probably afflicted with egoruptcy.

- Trying to impress others with how well he's doing. The more someone spouts off about his accomplishments, the less likely it is that he has accomplished much of anything.
- Constantly mouthing off about the deals he's working on.

- Dwelling on what he's accomplished in the past.

- Rapid expansion of offices (particularly if lavishly decorated), staff, or business in general.

- Talking incessantly about what he owns.

- Talking incessantly about who he knows.

When most or all of the above signs are evident, the patient's case of egoruptcy clearly is in its advanced stages and he has probably deteriorated beyond hope. Best you shield your face when passing him in order to avoid getting infected.

Zip the Lip

Feeding a big ego often takes the form of perpetual movement of the mouth and tongue. Big mistake. Concentrate, at all times, on being both quiet and patient. The safest way to operate is behind the scenes with a low profile. In my business, though publicity comes with the territory, I make it a point to be tight-lipped about my projects until they are completed.

There's seldom anything to gain by giving the world advance notice of your objectives. How many times have you jumped the gun and talked about your plans prematurely, only to be embarrassed when they fell through? If you manage to achieve your desired end, people will know about it soon enough. Additionally, you may even gain a reputation for being humble as a result of not shooting off your mouth about what you're working on.

The next time you're tempted to make an advance announcement to the world, remember that Murphy is out there waiting to trip you up. Even if you succeed in backing up your words, people will perceive you as a braggart. It's certainly not worth the risk of having a bunch of neurotic individuals jealously gnashing their teeth and doing everything possible to see to it that you end up dining on your own words some fine evening.

If Satan isn't alive and well on planet Earth, his chief aide certainly is. He's a little guy, with a sadistic smirk on his face, who carries

"Just keep running off at mouth, pal, and you'll be nursing a bad case of bursitis."

around a miniature pitchfork. The next time you shoot off your mouth about a plan you have in the works, quickly turn your head to the left. There you'll see him, sitting on your shoulder and whispering in your ear. He's none other than the Zip-the-Lip Leprechaun.

The Devil has assigned this homely little chap the task of urging incurable chatterboxes to let everyone know about their plans. Once he succeeds in getting you to run off at the mouth, he jams his pitchfork into your shoulder as his way of saying, "Gotcha!" His greatest delight comes in snatching defeat from victory at the last possible moment. The best way to let others know what you're going to do is to actually do it—*all the way through to completion*. The more confident you are that something good is about to happen, the less reason you have to risk putting your foot in your mouth. Your ego will be more than sufficiently assuaged, massaged, and patted *after* you have succeeded.

What I'm talking about here is a simple piece of advice contained in the **Zip-the-Lip Theory**, which states: *If you've got something good going, shut up!*

The nice thing is that the more you succeed, the more reason you have to feel secure, which should result in your having less of an urge to talk about your plans and more of a desire to produce results.

Billionaire Babies

You've undoubtedly known at least one person whose bloated ego manifested itself with endless talk about multimillion-dollar deals. However, many hotshots who reside in the USA's first space colony— Los Angeles—take it one step further. Tinseltown egomaniacs don't fool around with millions. Los Angeles is the home of the Billionaire Babies—guys who don't concern themselves with mere million-dollar-deal discussions. Yup, these are the flaky characters who like to talk in billions. The first time you encounter a Billionaire Baby, you assume he's just putting you on. But when you finally realize he's serious, you begin scoping the room for possible escape routes.

I once knew a seemingly intelligent Tinseltown guy who contracted a severe case of *Billionaire Babyitis*. He knew not one paltry millionaire. All the people in his deals were *billionaires*. At first, I thought it was just his way of figuratively expressing people's wealth. Ultimately, though, I became convinced that Tinselman actually believed there were carloads of billionaires running around loose on our planet—all of them dying to do deals with Southern California charlatans, of course.

On a number of occasions, I met some of the "billionaires" he had mentioned. One drove a classic Rolls Royce, which I later found out was on a month-to-month lease. Another one lived in a spectacular mansion, but it turned out that he was only a front for a group of investors who had put up the money to refurbish the estate with the intention of reselling it at a profit. And, of course, there was Mr. Bigspender, who was being chased all over town by collection agents.

I've known many wealthy people over the years—including a couple of *real* billionaires—and there's one thing they all seem to have in common: Not only do they not toss money around carelessly, they speak about it in reverent tones. A term like *billion* is not to be uttered cavalierly.

All this calls to mind the **B.S. Theory**, which states: *When you B.S others, you're merely being dishonest. But when you start believing your own B.S., bankruptcy is probably just around the corner.*

Megalomaniacs—people who suffer from delusions of grandeur—are hopelessly caught up in the B.S. Trap. Whenever you come in contact with such a self-delusive individual, don't stop to chat. Just smile, shake hands, bid him adieu, then walk as fast as you can in the other direction. A person who believes his own B.S. tends to make decisions based on the landfill of the mind, and anything anchored to landfill is doomed to crumble at the slightest sign of a tremor. Just make certain you're not around when the tremor occurs, because it can be extremely dangerous to your wealth.

Avoid getting intertwined in the B.S. neuroses of others, and, even more important, be vigilant about making certain it doesn't rub off on you. One of the best ways to accomplish this is by never trying to be something you're not, by diligently avoiding ego satisfactions, and by focusing on total honesty in both your words and actions.

Standing on Principle, Falling on Ego

It's also important not to get sidetracked by irrelevant challenges. Learn to disregard irritations that are unrelated to your main objective. More often than not, when someone makes a fuss over a relatively minor point, it's really just his ego getting in the way of his own best interests.

I prefer to avoid confrontations, mainly because they slow me down. If it's of monumental importance for the other guy to win a point that isn't relevant to my main objective, I'd just as soon give him the satisfaction. In fact, I'd prefer that we concentrate on nothing *but* nonessential points. Let the other guy believe he's winning the battle, while you remain focused on winning the war.

When you argue just for the sake of arguing, you're not acting in your rational self-interest. Your ego is in control, which means you're *out* of control.

The Fear Factor

If you try to motivate associates or subordinates by instilling fear in them, that, too, is probably a case of ego guiding your actions. Trying to rule out of fear is not in your best interest. It simply doesn't work over the long term, because those whom you think you have under control will be the very people who will fail to cooperate when you most need them. This is the centuries-old story of dictators being overthrown by their subjects. It's important to surround yourself with competent people, and competent people don't need to be controlled with an iron fist. As always, the best kind of associations are those that are voluntary.

THE ROAD TO RATIONAL DECISIONS

I've already alluded to the wisdom of seeking long-term solutions in lieu of short-term patching, and it's especially true when it comes to clearing the Financial Hurdle. Short-term patching is the catalyst for jumping from the frying pan into the fire, especially where money is concerned. When you have financial problems, your instincts often prod you to base your decisions on the expediency of the moment, which almost always makes matters worse.

The only way to build a solid foundation for financial success is to develop the self-discipline to think long term. Interestingly, long-term solutions usually turn out to be the most expedient solutions as well. In fact, I've come to refer to the long-term-solution approach as the "slow, fast way." By solving a problem on a permanent basis, it's over and done with. It may cause temporary discomfort and initially take a little longer, but the payoff is that you don't have to address the problem again down the road.

SELF-INTEREST

To clear the Financial Hurdle, it's important to focus on the reality of self-interest—not just yours, but that of everyone you're involved with. If there's nothing in it for the other guy, you may profit from him once, but in the long run you're going to lose him as a customer, client, or business associate—and, in the process, earn a bad reputation in the marketplace.

You should make it a special point to concern yourself with the desires of those who represent potential value to you. This is what the term *value for value* is all about, and I'm convinced it is still the most certain formula for success. There has to be something in it for the other person if you expect him to do business with you in the future. As a bonus, word will spread that you're a solid person to deal with, which will result in still more people wanting to do business with you.

Be straightforward and let the person on the other side of the negotiating table know that you're objective is to make the best possible deal you can, but *not* at the expense of losing a long-term relationship with him. A one-time killing will rarely reap as much as a lifetime of entering into mutually profitable deals with someone.

THE MIRACLE OF SIMPLICITY

Over the years, I have observed a peculiar human trait, succinctly summed up in the **Life-Complication Theory**, which states: *Human beings, by nature, tend to seek ways to complicate their lives. Given a choice between a simple and complicated method to accomplish an objective, most people will opt for the more complicated course of action.*

This is one of those great mysteries of life for which there is no logical explanation. It's a source of unending fascination to me to note the lengths to which individuals will go not only to seek out discomforting entanglements, but to invent ingenious methods to avoid eliminating existing complications from their lives.

This is especially true as it relates to clearing the Financial Hurdle. I am still amazed at the extent to which I went out of my way to complicate my business life when I was much younger. The time and money spent on building large organizations, setting up complex corporate structures, and becoming involved in deals from one coast to the other now seem incomprehensible to me. The result was that I never had time to engage in the one activity that is most likely to produce financial results: *creative thinking*. I was too busy working to carve out the time to think about making *serious* money.

Today, no one impresses me less than the guy who madly shuffles papers as he talks on the phone, periodically interrupts his conversation to blurt out orders to his secretary, and at the same time motions to a visitor to have a seat (with a wink that implies he'll "be with you in a minute"). It's been my experience that most successful people tend to make their way through their daily obligations in a calm, low-key manner.

Operating in a harried fashion can seriously decrease your odds of being around long enough to discover that money is only a means to an end. Further, as with crusades, there is weakness, not strength, in numbers. The larger the organization, the more people there are who have to be consulted before decisions can be made, thus the greater the opportunities for bureaucratic bungling, in-fighting, inefficiency, and confusion. That's why a small, efficient, well-run company can almost always beat a major corporation to the punch. The classic example of this is how Microsoft snuck up on, and surpassed, lethargic IBM. Big Blue never even saw Bill Gates and his cadre of nerds coming.

This is the main reason that giant corporations are usually the ones who fight for so-called antitrust and antimonopoly laws. The real purpose of such laws is to *protect* big business against smaller competitors who have an irritating habit of cutting into their profits.

I long ago lost my appetite for being a high-priced baby-sitter, which, for all practical purposes, is what you are when you have the responsibility of overseeing a large staff of people. It becomes a form of self-imprisonment. You have to think about everything you do, from the clothes you wear to what time you arrive at the office, because others are looking to you to set an example.

The same goes for travel. In the old days, I believed that the really great deals were in faraway places, usually on the other side of the continent. But it's amazing how many of those too-good-to-be true deals turned out to be illusions. As a result, I wasted an enormous amount of time and energy—not to mention thousands of dollars in unnecessary travel expenses—that could otherwise have been used for constructive projects that were easily accessible to me in my own back yard.

In this regard, my memory reaches back to some poignant scenes from an old movie, *Fanny*, in which the main character of the same name was played by Leslie Carone. In the film, Fanny is desperately in love with a young man named Marius, and he with her. Fanny wants Marius to marry her, but Marius, in his words, is "so divided—so torn."

Marius relates to Fanny a story an old seaman had told him when he was just a boy. The mariner vividly described "the isles beneath the winds where black trees grow," saying that "when you cut them they are gold inside, and smell of camphor and pepper. That's when it happened," Marius continues, his eyes glimmering with excitement, "this deep, painful wish I have. And when I see a boat steaming out of the harbor, it makes me dizzy, as though I were falling forward always . . . toward the sea."

So Marius, despite his deep love for Fanny, goes off to sea in search of the wonders the old mariner had described. More than a year later, he returns home for a brief visit and calls on Fanny, who has by then married another man. In a dramatic scene, Fanny asks Marius if he had seen "the isles beneath the winds," and Marius, in a somber tone, replies affirmatively.

"What were they like?" Fanny further inquires.

With a sad and wistful look in his eyes, Marius responds, "Have you ever seen photographs of the craters of the moon? That's what they were like—volcanic ash. Oh, Fanny, I left with such high hopes."

The moral is that it's very easy to get carried away by the illusion of greener grass on the other side of the fence. When it comes to business dealings, those isles beneath the winds all too often turn out to be nothing more than volcanic ash. It's remarkable how much more efficient you can be in your own office—especially in this day and age of the Internet—than on an airplane or in a hotel room.

Another key aspect of simplicity is to rid yourself of involvement with big institutions. When I was the head of a public company, I spent a majority of my time either talking to, or doing paperwork for, bureaucrats at the American Stock Exchange, the SEC (Swift Execution Commission), and banks, on top of having to constantly appease directors, securities dealers, and stockholders. The main job of most high-level public company executives is to comply with regulations—mostly government regulations. That translates into mountains of paperwork, endless meetings with attorneys and accountants, and strategizing with fellow executives on how to appease this ever-expanding army of busybodies. With all the inherent wasted time and energy involved, I'm in awe of any high-level executive of a public company who is able to find the time to work on creating better products and services for his company's customers.

Beware the Sheiks

Being a writer has taught me the importance of not becoming sidetracked, regardless of how appealing an opportunity may appear to be. There is much wisdom in General Patton's advice about single-mindedness and relentlessly striving toward your main objective.

As I said in Chapter 1, no one can have all the candy in the store, and the sooner you face up to that reality, the sooner you can focus on the business of making money instead of bringing chaos into your life. Through the years, I've managed to develop the self-discipline to concentrate on one deal at a time and leave all the other deals to the rest of the world's entrepreneurs. For the past two decades, my motto has been: Success means doing what you do best and letting others do the rest.

It's also important to be highly selective about the deals you work on. There simply are too many "ifs" and "buts" and "maybes" in most deals. Worst of all, too many deals require becoming involved with a lot of people, and one of your main objectives should be to deal with as few people as possible. People problems complicate your life, and complications mean roadblocks between you and the freedom that lies on the other side of the Financial Hurdle.

When I was a master at complicating my life, every over-hyped deal in the world seemed to find its way to my desk—condominiums in the Mojave Desert, bank charters in Aruba, a process for converting cow dung into bricks in Bombay—you name it. Whatever it was, I probably saw it—and probably seriously considered it.

Then there were the sheiks. I still have nightmares about those waves of sheiks coming at me—wearing Armani suits and Arabian head scarves and boasting about all the "Arab oil money" they claimed to represent. The result? After years spent looking at, and working on, hundreds of deals, I never once saw any Arab oil money change hands. Maybe such exotic capital is out there somewhere, but, if so, you can be certain it is changing hands on a level that is far above your head and mine. The Saudi royal family has all the bases covered. They hardly need you or me to come up with safe and lucrative places for parking their money.

Though Americans are way out front when it comes to the number of flakes per square foot of geography, we certainly don't have a monopoly on con men. The Arabs, Indians, and Chinese all have more than their fair share of flakes. Because we live in a world of delusions, a person's status as an expert (along with his air of legitimacy) tends to increase in direct proportion to the distance he travels from his home country—especially if has a white scarf wrapped around his head and is wearing a three-piece suit. Bottom line: All other things being equal, it's a good idea to focus on simple deals close to home. Don't allow yourself to get sidetracked by every exotic deal that comes floating by, no matter how the guy presenting it is dressed.

Remember, creative thinking is the most important of all business activities, and the more you simplify your life, the more time you will have to engage in it. Resist the temptation to be an around-the-clock wheeler-dealer. You can make more money than you can ever hope to spend without reviewing every deal that's circulating in the flake network. A frenetic life only succeeds in cluttering your mind, and a cluttered mind is self-defeating. Profit is directly related to the number of uncluttered, creative hours one is able to carve out of his daily schedule.

TAKING HOLD OF THE WHEEL

If there's one thing that makes me nervous, it's sitting in the passenger seat of a car. Though I dislike driving, I do so because I like being in control. I have repeatedly emphasized the importance of acting out of choice rather than chance, and that's possible only if you're in control of your actions. While it's true that there are endless factors in life that are beyond your control, it's also true that there are many areas of life over which you do have control.

First and foremost, you have the power to control your awareness. No one can prevent you from being alert and rational. People often fail to concentrate on what's going on around them. Which is unfortunate, because the best opportunities often drift into your life when you're least expecting them. In addition, people are often too focused on some misfortune they have endured to recognize the opportunities that continually cross their path. And of the few who do recognize those opportunities, only a small percentage have the alertness and/or courage to move quickly enough to take advantage of them.

On the other hand, there will always be that small fraction of the population that is not only aware, but ready and willing to step up to the plate and take advantage of any opportunity that comes their way. The person who is prepared doesn't need much of an opening to take action.

People who see themselves as victims of bad luck have a difficult time understanding that the surest road to success is to create one's own breaks. Sadly, most of them are victims of the **Waiting-to-Be-Discovered Theory**, which states: *If you're waiting for something to happen, you're not in control of your destiny. Don't wait for something to happen; make it happen!*

Self-Discipline

Self-discipline is the essence of self-control. It results in an efficient use of one's time, which in turn results in more time for creative endeavors. There will always be an abundance of distractions around you—the lure of the opposite sex, phone calls, spectator sports, television—so it's up to you not to allow such distractions to guide your life. Of primary importance in this regard is to learn how to say no—both to people and activities.

When it comes to self-discipline, you have to be careful not to delude yourself. For example, people often try to convince themselves that certain social gatherings are helpful to their business. Personally, I've always been skeptical of the efficacy of cocktail parties, golf matches, and business lunches. Based on firsthand experience, I believe that the most meaningful business progress is made when talking face to face with someone in his or my office. While the other guy is exchanging off-color jokes with a prospect over a three-martini lunch, I prefer to be in a more serious setting where all the parties can more easily focus on business.

THE CONFUSION CRUTCH

Whether it's a career decision or how to handle a specific financial problem, you should always be careful when it comes to accepting the advice of others. Listening to too many opinions can be fatal to your financial aspirations.

Every industry has its Discouragement Fraternity—people who go to great lengths to try to convince you that you can't make it in their field. Because of their own insecurity, consciously or unconsciously they are prepared to do anything within their power to prevent you from ever getting out of the starting gate. The reason for this is that you represent competition to them.

Their implied message is, "How dare you be so presumptuous as to think you can succeed in this business when you have no experience—which we're trying to prevent you from gaining by convincing you that you shouldn't come into this business in the first place." The reality is that you have to start somewhere. It's like a banker who won't consider you for a loan until you can prove you don't need it.

Do yourself a favor and don't expect others in the industry of your choice to help you get started. On the contrary, assume that there is an army of neurotic individuals out there who will go to great lengths to put obstacles in your path. Never forget that no one owes you anything, and rest assured they know it. It's up to you and you alone to decide when you're ready to make the move into your chosen field. You don't need so-called credentials; you don't need the approval of others; you don't need the crutch of reassurance from friends. All you need is to be ready, and you are the best judge of when that is. If you believe your time has arrived, ignore the negative input of the Discouragement Fraternity and boldly move forward without regard to what anyone else thinks.

PLAYING YOUR OWN GAME

It's not what you say or do that counts, but what your posture is when you say or do it. There's no question that a person can exercise a great deal of control over his own posture. Someone else may have more financial strength than you, but he cannot force you to play by his rules without your consent. A rational man, said Ayn Rand, "never leaves his interests at the mercy of any one person or single, specific concrete. He may need clients, but not any one particular client—he may need a job, but not any one particular job."

People often think of this as bluffing, but you're not bluffing if you really mean what you say. Personally, I make it a point never to bluff. I'm careful about throwing out ultimatums to people, because once I do, I follow through. You can only afford to throw down the gauntlet if you're good at what you do. If you don't bring value to the table, being tough is an exercise in futility.

Once you decide how *you* want to play the game, your first task should be to pick the right person or persons with whom to play it. It's easy to have things your way against a weak opponent, but the tougher the opposition, the more vigilant you have to be when it comes to setting the tempo and guidelines. The strength of your posture will to a great extent depend upon the parties with whom you choose to deal, which in turn will go a long way toward determining your success.

In particular, if you're having financial difficulties, don't try to play in the big leagues. When you're operating from a position of financial weakness, the tone of your voice and the look in your eyes give you away. If you can't afford to lose, it's not only hard to hide your financial weakness, it's difficult to make rational decisions—and almost impossible to avoid being intimidated by financially stronger opponents.

If at times you have no choice but to be involved with someone who's on a much higher financial level than you, there are two weapons that can help you control the situation. The first is to make certain you're good at your craft. If it's obvious that you're someone who can create value, the other person will respect you even if you don't have staying power. As a result, he may be willing to deal with you—for reasons of pure self-interest—without using strong-arm tactics.

Ironically, the second weapon works best when you're destitute. Even in those bad old days in Beverly Hills, when I was groveling around on all fours and nursing my leper sores, I came to the conclusion that I still had one advantage over most of the opposition: I had everything to gain and nothing to lose. Because I knew I was at the very bottom, I took a strong stance when it came to drawing the line on not being pushed around or allowing anyone to intimidate me.

It's also a good idea to remember this principle when you are the one with the upper hand. Never push the other person so far that he has nothing to lose, because he might just decide to jump off a financial cliff and pull you along with him.

GETTING PAID

There's nothing more frustrating than putting 110 percent effort into one deal after another and consistently ending up on the short end of the stick. Remember, no matter how well you perform, your efforts are only a means to an end—*getting paid.* Your main focus should always be on the *precise method* by which funds will be transferred from *someone else's* bank account into *yours.* This seemingly simple proposition almost never happens by accident, and almost never without resistance on the part of the party who is supposed to pay you. To underscore the importance of what I've just said, it's the only sentence in this entire book that I'm not only going to repeat, but repeat in bold italics: ***This seemingly simple proposition almost never happens by accident, and almost never without resistance on the part of the party who is supposed to pay you.*** To be forewarned is to be forearmed.

Should you come to the conclusion that you can't control the payment of monies due you, then the only solution is to bypass the person who is supposed to pay you and take matters into your own hands. Think of it as the **Sure Theory**, which states: *The only way you can be certain that your objective will be accomplished is to take matters into your own hands and not expect any help from anyone.* This kind of independent mind-set puts you in control of your own destiny. When you count on outside help, you're *out* of control.

One final but important note on this subject: *Checks don't count until the funds have cleared the bank!*

MONEY GAME TACTICS

One of the things that makes winning in the business world so difficult is that every player brings a different repertoire of tactics to the game, which means you can't wed yourself to any one strategy. The only thing you should assume will never change is that everyone you deal with will act in his own self-interest at all times. Whether or not you or I choose to acknowledge this reality is irrelevant. Remember, realities exist irrespective of what we choose to believe. If you refuse to accept this basic reality of human nature, you have no hope for long-term success even if you do everything else right.

Let me make it clear that I am in no way advocating an anything-goes philosophy. On the contrary, the most rational way to look out for one's own best interest is to focus on creating value for others. But that doesn't mean you can count on everyone else being as enlightened as you are on the subject of value creation. Also, always keep in mind that when someone does create value for you, he is still acting in his own self-interest. It just means he understands that helping you get what you want is the best way to get what he wants. It's this kind of motivation—enlightened self-interest—that drives the free market.

Financialese

You should make every effort to learn the language of the Money Game—Financialese—in order to correctly interpret the remarks of other players. Some translation examples of Financialese include:

Statement: Don't worry about a thing.

Translation: You'd better start worrying about *everything*.

Statement: Let me know if there's anything I can do to help.

Translation: Don't bother me.

Statement: I would never do anything dishonest. Life is too short to make enemies.

Translation: I'll do whatever it takes to get the best of you. Life is too short to *worry* about making enemies.

Statement: My reputation is beyond reproach. You can check me out with my bank.

Translation: I've managed to accumulate a lot of money by shafting guys like you who were stupid enough to believe that all they needed to do was check me out with my bank.

Of course, not every opponent who crosses your path will be speaking Financialese, but it's prudent to assume he is. By doing so, if it turns out that Financialese is his native tongue, you won't be left standing in your Jockey shorts, scratching your head and trying to figure out what happened to your clothes.

The Cash-Flow Game

The object of the Cash-Flow Game is to use the other guy's cash for as long as possible. Big corporations and wealthy individuals understand the truth embodied in the **Financial Geometric-Growth Theory**, which states: *Money tends to grow exponentially in smart hands, the end result being that the rich get richer.*

Consider the following list of good things that the cash-rich individual or company has going for him/it:

- Excess cash can be put to work in the best combination of low risk, high yield investments that can earn the investor still more cash.

- Cash tends to draw the best people and best deals to those who are known to have lots of it.

- Cash provides staying power, an intangible that all too often is the difference between success and failure.

- The cash-rich individual is more likely to make sound, rational decisions.

- Cash can be leveraged, often without its owner having to put up any money at all. As the legendary Meshulam Riklis used to point out when he was building his McCrory Corp. empire, the intelligent use of a cash-rich balance sheet can produce a river of additional cash—what he referred to as "the effective nonuse of cash."

The point is that cash begets cash, but in ways that are not understood by, and not visible to, the average person. The only limitation to how much can be made from a cache of cash is the creativity of the individual who possesses it. In the words of Stuart Wilde: "The secret to money is having some."

Unfortunately, this theory works in reverse as well. When you're squeezed for cash, bad things tend to happen. Consider:

- When word gets around that you're in financial trouble, good deals no longer find their way to your desk.

- With a lack of staying power, you're always dealing from a position of weakness.

- You're likely to make scared money decisions—an example of short term patching—instead of sound decisions based on a long-term perspective.

- You have no leverage, and, as a result, no one is willing to lend you money or invest in you.

- You have to spend an enormous amount of time and energy putting out fires, while cash-rich opponents spend their time thinking of creative ways to increase their cash positions.

Comparing the two possible ways in which geometric growth can work, it's not hard to understand why savvy players place such a big emphasis on cash. It would be difficult to think of a unique cash-flow scheme, because the world's largest corporations have already thought of every conceivable way to get their hands on the other guy's cash—interest free.

The so-called security deposit paid to owners of rental properties is an old favorite. So, too, is the non-interest-bearing checking account (wherein banks usually make *you* pay a service charge for allowing them to have the free use of *your* money). And many basic monthly charges, such as Internet services, are billed in advance, *before* the customer actually uses the service for the period being billed.

American Express bluntly refers to its version of the Cash-Flow Game as "the float." The company sells travelers checks to people, knowing that an average of sixty-five days will elapse between the time they are purchased and the time the buyer cashes the checks. During that sixty-five-day period, a large percentage of the cash is invested in safe instruments such as tax-exempt municipal bonds.

You may not have the power to employ the cash-flow schemes of giant corporations, but you can still use this valuable principle to your advantage on a smaller scale. Always proceed from the axiom that every day that someone else's money is in your pocket, you are that much ahead of the game. Likewise, every day that *your* money is in *someone else's* pocket, you are losing the use of that cash, along with all the benefits it can provide you via the Financial Geometric-Growth Theory. To the extent it can be avoided, never relinquish cash without putting up a fight. Be vigilant about trying to hang on to as many chips as possible for the longest possible period of time.

LEGALMAN: THE GAME'S MASTER CROUPIER

In a rational, ethical world, Legalman would never have even been allowed on the playing field. Unfortunately, we don't live in a rational, ethical world. In any event, it's too late, because Legalman is already solidly entrenched as one of the game's legitimate players.

Legalman is that lecherous subspecies of Homo sapiens who dashes onto the scene in the closing stages of your deal—brandishing his satchelful of little deal-killing goodies—just in time to bring everything to a screeching halt. The first thing he says is something like, "I want you to know that I'm not one of those deal-killing attorneys, so you can relax. It's up to my victim (er, client) to make his own decisions." (Translation: "The only way this deal is going to close is over my dead body. Heh . . . heh . . . heh.")

Legalman plays his certification role to the hilt. He's the classic expert, the guy who can tell you all the reasons why you can't do something. In his case, it's not a matter of trying to convince you that you're incapable; rather, he either implies that there is a mysterious legal reason why something you want to do can't be done or suggests that it would be a bad business move on your part. How Legalman managed to get into the game as a business expert, in addition to an interpreter of the law, has always mystified me.

Legalman also has been endowed with incredible gall. He not only got into the game without bringing anything but his law degree to the table, but managed to finesse his way into the role of chief skimmer. While the suckers roll the dice, Legalman, like a croupier at a crap table, relentlessly rakes his take off the top. Technically, of course, he refers to his skimming tactics as "legal fees," insisting that he is providing a legitimate service for his client. To put it in more gentle terms, one might say that all he is guilty of is taking money from the other players in the game in exchange for creating problems for them.

Whatever words you choose to describe this phenomenon, the result is the same: Over the long haul, what Legalman really accomplishes is to redistribute chips from the pockets of legitimate players into his own. The name of the game from Legalman's standpoint is to keep the hostilities flying back and forth, stir up endless litigation, and drag out every confrontation as long as possible. Time is always on Legalman's side, because each day that the fighting continues is another day that he has the opportunity to rake chips onto his pile with his nifty croupier's stick. Mercifully, once he's pilfered the last bit of gold from all the other players' teeth, he picks up his little bag of deal-killing goodies, spreads his cape, and disappears into the suburbs to enjoy his evening martini(s).

Carl Sandburg described it best when he asked:

> *When the lawyers are through*
> *What is there left . . . ?*
> *Can a mouse nibble at it*
> *And find enough to fasten a tooth in?*

"Don't be shy, boys. Step right up to the table and keep the hostilities going."

Great Legalman Myths

One of the main reasons Legalman is able to get by with such outrageous and avaricious behavior is that he has succeeded in enshrouding himself in a cloud of mystery. He relies heavily on the government-protection racket for the legal profession (i.e., only those with government-approved licenses are granted permission to carry a croupier's stick). The naïve and easily intimidated misconstrue this to mean that only Legalman has a thorough understanding of the law and that it is beyond the comprehension of mere laymen.

Which, of course, is nonsense. Yet, millions of people continue to believe that the services Legalman performs are sacred and that his government-approved monopoly gives him some sort of mystical powers of understanding that you and I can never hope to acquire. The truth, of course, is that you can get a divorce, form a corporation, and even die without the aid of Legalman. Aside from Legalman's tendency to be lazy, negligent, and incompetent, my experience with him is that he has great difficulty just trying to draft an intelligible sentence. Because of the latter defect, many years ago I decided to take matters into my own hands and draft my own contracts. That's the only way I could be confident that everyone involved would actually be able to understand what was agreed upon.

The Adventures of Legalboy

Then there's the myth about Legalman's innate superior intelligence. Sorry, but my firsthand encounters with Legalman have convinced me that, as a group, attorneys are a bit on the dull side. In this regard, I vividly recall an experience I had with an early evolutionary form of Legalman, commonly referred to as *Legalboy*. Legalboy was one of those self-delusive little twits who had only recently snuck into the game, fresh out of his final course in law school and brimming over with Perry Mason fantasies. Having gotten top grades in Circumcision 401, 2, and 3, he was eager to begin wielding the spanking-new, pink croupier's stick his family had given him as a graduation gift.

Of course, sophisticated players in the Money Game usually just ignore Legalboy. True, they might engage in an occasional chuckle or two as they watch him running around in his $150 three-piece polyester suit and shouting incoherent legal phrases at anyone who will listen. But, for the most part, they don't really acknowledge his existence.

Even so, if Legalboy is persistent enough, he will eventually find a few naïve souls willing to listen to his gibberish, which is how he begins the arduous task of building a client list. In this particular case, one of those naïve souls happened to be a creditor of mine from my Beverly Hills leprosy days. He had obtained a default judgment against me in the amount of $24,000, because at the time he filed suit against me, I was in such dire financial straits that I couldn't afford to defend myself. I only owed his client $8,000, but the law allows a plaintiff to file for treble damages. Meaning that when you're sued, there is an added penalty for being so poor that you can't afford legal fees. That's right—if you can't afford to defend yourself, you have to pay three times the actual amount of your debt.

Somehow or other, my creditor had stumbled upon Legalboy at just about the time I was starting to take significant steps up the financial ladder. He explained to this giant of jurisprudence that he had already obtained a judgment, but hadn't been able to collect on it. Which is all Legalboy needed to hear to shift into his go-get-'em routine. He immediately started calling me several times a day and bombarding me with the silliest threats imaginable. Like any overzealous cubby, his manner of speech was rapid and incoherent.

My adversary completely bought into Legalboy's dramatic performance and played the role of mesmerized client to the hilt. It was Legalboy's moment in the sun, and he was loving every minute of it. With his confidence increasing daily, he relentlessly pressed forward with his "Just watch me nail this tortoise" routine.

Legalboy knew where my office was, so he could have served me with judgment/debtor papers at any time. To my pleasant surprise, however, he didn't. My only guess as to why he failed to take this incredibly easy step was that he must have done exceptionally well in Negligence 401 when he was in law school. Had he taken the trouble to serve me, he would have quickly discovered that all the money I possessed—about $100,000—was in a checking account at a bank right next door to my office! Then, all he would have needed to do was walk into the bank with the sheriff, and in five minutes they would have handed him $24,000—the treble-damages amount—in cash. (My creditor was no longer willing to accept the $8,000 I actually owed him. Nope, he wanted the $24,000 treble-damages amount, and that just didn't fit in with my moral code.)

Of course, even in those pre-computer days, any entrepreneur worth his salt could find out, in a day or two, in what bank or banks any person in his home town had accounts. But you don't learn simple, real-world skills like that in law school. You learn them by actively participating in the Money Game—for the most part through adversity. Since Legalboy lacked experience and possessed a cerebral mass the size of a pea, he apparently didn't know how to go about such a routine procedure. Luckily for me, he didn't even take the trouble to serve papers on the bank right next door to my office, which was the most obvious place to start searching for money. He was too wrapped up in his hard-nosed-negotiations performance to take any meaningful action on behalf of his client.

From the outset of this little financial skirmish, I had figured that, considering my vulnerability, it would be a bargain if I could settle the matter for something in the area of $13,000. But when it was all over, Legalboy, who had put on an absolutely brilliant performance for his entranced client, ended up nailing The Tortoise for the grand sum of $10,000. Not in cash, mind you, but in monthly installments over a period of a year! A great example of how even someone in my then-vulnerable position could find a way to win at the Cash-Flow Game. Considering that I had the

use of varying percentages of the $10,000 for up to a year, there is no question that I came out far better than if I had agreed to pay the original $8,000 in one lump sum to Legalboy's client.

After the settlement was signed, Legalboy bristled with pride until I feared the plastic buttons on his vest would pop off and ruin his image. His client was in utter awe. "How in the world do these legal brains do it?" he must have been thinking. I guess it's just as well he never knew that Legalboy had just *cost* him $14,000 by not being competent enough to simply walk into the bank next door to my office and get him more than twice the amount of the eventual settlement—*in cash*—without having to go through his ferocious cubby routine.

What's nice about this true story is that everyone got what he wanted. Legalboy raked in a fee for *costing* his client money, solidified his relationship with his client, and, of prime importance, got his ego massaged. The comatose client believed justice had been done and that he had succeeded in collecting a debt that was owed to him, apparently finding a way to rationalize the fact that he had ended up with only about 40 percent of the face amount of the judgment—less croupier's fees, of course. With "victory" in hand, he could then go on to help perpetuate some of the most widely accepted Legalman (and Legalboy) myths.

The Tortoise, of course, was the happiest of all. Not only did I save $14,000—$14,000 that a sharper version of Legalboy could easily have snatched from my bank account—I also gained the use of varying percentages of the $10,000 settlement money, interest free, over a period of one year. If you have a little vino handy, a toast is in order: Long live Legalboy!

Defending Against the Croupier's Stick

If you're one of the legitimate players in the Money Game, you should make it a high priority to minimize the effects of Legalman whenever and wherever possible. The first step toward achieving this end is to wake up to the reality that Legalman is just an average schmo—er, Joe—with a croupier's license who is highly skilled at perpetuating myths about himself and his "services."

It's also important to get it out of your head that everything is a legal problem. Over a period of time, I came to realize that most of my legal problems weren't legal problems at all. They were just *problems*, problems that I could resolve much better myself—at no cost. It ultimately became clear to me that, more often than not, so-called legal problems began to appear *after* Legalman entered the picture. The original problem between two parties usually becomes relegated to a minor status with the advent of the new, more serious problems that Legalman manages to introduce into virtually every situation.

Through experience, I became quite good at anticipating the kinds of "problems" that Legalman was adept at injecting into an otherwise harmonious situation, and I put a great deal of effort into trying to head him off at the pass. I did this by addressing potential phantom problems before he even had a chance to bring them up. And when I discussed them, I never talked in terms of "problems." Instead, I referred to them as "items to be taken care of," and I saw it as my job to follow through and take care of such items.

Unfortunately, your resistance to using Legalman is only half the battle, because the other party to your deal may decide to call him in unilaterally. And when that happens, it almost always spells trouble. If, for example, you sell real estate or insurance for a living, you know that the appearance of Legalman can all too often result in your sale falling apart at the eleventh hour. In businesses like these, where it's hard to keep Legalman out of the fray, your best bet is to try to out-finesse him. However, even when you become skilled at doing so, he's still going to succeed a good deal of the time, so never make the mistake of underestimating him. Legalman is normally very good at his chosen profession—*deal killing*—so stay alert at all times.

Of course, the ideal is to be in a business where you don't have to become involved with people who are so unsophisticated that they think it's illegal to consummate a transaction without Legalman's approval. I believe it's more than just a coincidence that I've closed some of the biggest deals of my life without Legalman's input. It's also instructive to note that in every one of those deals, the other party not only was sophisticated, but wanted to conclude the deal as much as I did. Thus, sophistication and a high level of motivation are two keys worth looking for when searching for makeable deals. It's the unsophisticated individual who is most likely to call in Legalman and allow himself to be worked into a tizzy by artificially created problems.

I cannot deny that there are times when you may actually need Legalman, but you should exhaust all other avenues before you resort to bringing him into the picture. Allowing Legalman out of his cage should be looked upon as a measure of last resort. And when and if you do have to call on him, be prepared for a long, drawn-out battle. Also, check your bank balance because the billing damages are likely to be worse than your original legal problem.

All this firsthand experience with Legalman can be summed quite simply up in the **Legalman Proper-Use Theory**, which states: *There is only one kind of situation in which Legalman's services are valuable to a client—when the client has decided he wants to back out of a deal he has already agreed to, but is too embarrassed to say so. Legalman can make it happen!*

All other things being equal, if you're serious about achieving a high percentage rate when it comes to closing deals, your best bet is to lock Legalman in his cage and throw away the key.

UNCLE SAM: THE ONLY PLAYER WHO PLAYS WITH GUNS

With the government, you have a problem of a completely different dimension. While Legalman sneaks into the game under the fence and uses a croupier's stick to grab your chips, the government uses force to invite itself in. That puts all the other players at a decided disadvantage, because it's hard to maneuver around a bullet.

Of course, the average Magoo or Ostrich doesn't see, or refuses to see, the reality that the government uses the threat of force to get what it wants. There are many reasons for his detachment from reality. One is that he is intimidated through custom and tradition into blindly cooperating with those in positions of power. Second, he is often intimidated into peaceful cooperation through the government's use of slogans—particularly patriotic slogans. Finally, the government's monopoly on the use of force is what allows it to maintain control through the unspoken threat of violence without its actually having to employ such force.

It's no wonder that an "anything-goes" attitude prevails in business when you consider that one of the players is allowed to use guns to steal from everyone else in the game. Seen in this light, the Financial Hurdle becomes a game played by you and your competitors, using your wits and skills to make money by creating better products and services, while at the same time trying to protect your assets from that greatest of all robber barons—the government.

Never deceive yourself by ignoring the reality that the government is your chief adversary when it comes to getting ahead financially. All your competitors combined are not as formidable a foe as government, simply because they are not allowed to use force against you. One time, loud and clear: When it comes to your financial well-being, the government is not your friend; it is your worst enemy.

Government Mythology: A Study in Word Usage

Compared to the mystique behind which the government has managed to hide, myths about Legalman are rather mild. It's amazing what can be done when political thugs have virtually unlimited money to spend on propaganda. And through the phenomenon of gradualism, the propaganda becomes accepted by most of the sleepwalking public.

Another clever use of words is demonstrated by the fact that the government itself is thought of as a living entity by millions of otherwise rational individuals. But the government does not have wants, needs, desires, and emotions of its own. The word *government* is nothing more than a label given to a group of individuals who draw paychecks from the public trough and wield virtually unchecked power over those (citizens) who pay their salaries.

One of the reasons government acts in a conglomeration of contradictory ways, and why virtually everything it attempts to do ends in colossal failure, is the very fact that it is *not* a living entity. As a result, the most powerful politicians and bureaucrats, acting in their own self-interests, are constantly struggling against one another, vying for ever more power and trying to bring about "legislation" which *they* desire.

To think of the government as some sort of sacred entity is to believe that the *human beings* who actually comprise it are sacred. Of course, many people cherish the government because they see it as a means to their personal ends. But the government is not a means to an end for the individual whose objective is to look out for Number One and who finds it contemptible to violate the rights of others.

The question is, if what the government has to offer is so great for the individual, why must it use force to get people to go along with its programs? The obvious answer is that what the government offers is *not* great; it is restraint of freedom. The practical consequences of government are that it uses the threat of violence either to:

1. Force you to do something you do not want to do;

2. Force you to stop doing something you *do* want to do; or

3. Force you to give up something that's rightfully yours.

Setting the Example for an "Anything-Goes" Society

Then there's the mythology of "law." Aside from the fact that the government's use of force creates an anything-goes society, its laws set a bad example for the masses. It's a case of monkey see, monkey do. If Big Brother can legally confiscate the assets of individuals, force them into kill-or-be-killed situations (patriotically referred to as *war*), interfere with their sex lives, and commit thousands of other violations of natural rights, you can't blame the poor guy who's just trying to make ends meet for having an anything-goes attitude as well.

You don't have to have a very high level of awareness to realize that one doesn't prove that a law is right or moral merely by stating that it *is* a law. The only relevant consideration with regard to government laws is whether or not they are in violation of Natural Law and natural rights. Academicians have used various terms to define Natural Law and natural rights, but I believe they can be summed up rather simply: Every man possesses a natural right to pursue his own happiness in any way he so chooses, and retain ownership over *all* the fruits of his labor, so long as he does not forcibly interfere with the same rights in others.

To say that laws are necessary to protect individuals sounds great until you realize that most laws interfere with the freedom of individuals—particularly the endless number of absurd victimless-crime laws on the books. How can any group of people—whether it goes by the name of *government* or any other moniker—know what's good for you when you have desires, ambitions, needs, beliefs, and standards that are different from those of anyone else? How can others act in your best interest when they don't even know you? Only you can decide what's best for you, and anyone who tries to do it for you, especially by utilizing force, is an aggressor and is in violation of Natural Law.

No matter what kind of wording you employ in an attempt to ignore the facts, the truth always remains: Government restrains you, and restraint violates Natural Law. And when it comes to your financial well-being, that restraint manifests itself as a barrier that keeps you from transacting business freely in the marketplace, which is why government is the biggest obstacle to your clearing the Financial Hurdle.

How Formidable Is the Government as an Opponent?

All government does to you is:

- Steal a large portion of your personal income;

- Close the doors to your business if you don't fork over a specified percentage of your profits;

- Make the money you do retain worth less every day by printing currency with no backing behind it;

- Charge you rent for living in the home you thought you owned (euphemistically referred to as "property taxes");

- Tell you what minimums you have to pay your employees and whom you must hire;

- Dictate what you can charge for your products and services (through price controls handed down by the FTC);

- Pass judgment on what products you can sell (through the FDA);

- And, the real coup de grace, make it illegal for you to compete against its own poorly run monopolies (such as the United States Postal Service).

A walk through Central Park at midnight is safer than having benevolent government watching over you.

Defending against the Monster

Over the past several decades, thanks in great part to our modern information age, government's mystique and sanctity have been rapidly eroding. The facts are becoming too noticeable in your pocketbook, your home, and in many other aspects of your life. Is there any way to put an end to this aggression? Not completely, but you can certainly do a number of things to hinder the government's ability to squash your efforts to succeed.

For one, always start from the assumption that if you come up with a way to make a profit by creating a product or service that the market values, sooner or later the government will try to make it illegal. In other words, circumstances will continually change. If you accept this reality, you're in a much better position to move in another direction when the rules shift.

Always make a concerted effort to avoid as much contact with the government as possible. It drives the power holders crazy when they don't have a means of keeping tabs on your day-to-day activities. But even with their millions of employees, drones, and Internet-snooping techniques, they can't watch over everyone around the clock.

In order to compensate for this deficiency in the system, they've set up a network of regulatory agencies and commissions, the number and scope of which are staggering. These bodies (e.g., the SEC, FTC, FCC, FDA,CAB) are, of course, unconstitutional in every respect. But from the standpoint of looking out for number one, that's irrelevant, because the fact is that they exist whether or not you or I like it. Remember, our objective is to find the best ways to deal with reality rather than trying to change things over which we have little or no control.

All of these agencies are headed by nonelected bureaucrats who have virtual carte blanche to make or break any individual or company. More often than not, their arbitrary regulations see to it that competition is eliminated, which protects giant corporations and guarantees that consumers will pay higher prices for inferior products and services than they would in a free market.

If you're in business for yourself, my best advice to you regarding government is to try to pick an industry or occupation that's regulated as little as possible. And if you're already in a heavily regulated business and don't believe it's practical to get out, the best thing you can do is keep a low profile and stay out of the way of applicable regulatory agencies. Never take regulatory agencies on head-to-head. You'll only be wasting valuable time, energy, and money. The deck is stacked against you from the start, so that even if you win in court, the Feds will see to it that you lose down the road.

Finally, even if you do manage to stay out of an industry or occupation not presently burdened with a strong-arm government oversight agency, you should still operate on the assumption that such will not always be the case. It's always wise to keep in mind the Changing-Circumstances Theory and be prepared to make your move when busybody government hacks decide to step in and starting changing the rules of the game.

MURPHY'S GHOST

Finally, there is the player you can always count on to disrupt your best-laid plans—the ghost of Old Man Murphy. As I previously stated, Murphy doesn't discriminate. He's happy to inject problems into just about anyone's life in a wide variety of areas—including love, friendship, and health—but nothing is quite as exhilarating to him as causing people to trip over the Financial Hurdle. Being a ghost, he is, of course, invisible, but the problems he creates to thwart your every financial move are not.

Can you do anything to stop him? You certainly can't fight something you can't see, so the only answer is to try to prepare yourself for his inevitable appearances at the worst possible time. I believe that all Old Man Murphy really wants is a little respect. It's only when you start getting overconfident and assuming that you have everything under control—when you can't see how anything can possibly go wrong—that you raise Murphy's ire and are in danger of having him hand you your head in a ziplock bag. The truth is that he's a relatively docile ghost, so long as you heed his law.

Perhaps you're one of those people whom Murphy has treated so shabbily that you haven't even been able to get out of the starting gate. If so, don't despair. He's just testing your mettle. A wise, elderly gentleman once told me, after I had long tried in vain to clear the Financial Hurdle, that once you get the hang of it—once you start making money—riches come so quickly, and in such great abundance, that you wonder why you had so much trouble succeeding all those years. At the time, I found his remarks hard to believe, but firsthand experience has proven to my satisfaction that he was absolutely right.

ONCE YOU'VE GOT IT

Let's assume, for the moment, that you've finally managed to clear the Financial Hurdle, meaning you've achieved enough financial success to do as you please. Now what? Should you just kick back and relax? To do so, as many have found, is a surefire formula for boredom and unhappiness. So even after you've achieved financial success, there's ongoing work to be done if your objective is to look out for number one.

For starters, it's important to your long-term happiness not to allow money to change you into something you're not, which means you must be vigilant about advertising the real you to the rest of the world. Once you get on top financially, your ego should require a lot less nourishment, so there's no need to put on airs. If you start taking yourself too seriously, you are tempting the financial abyss to pull you down again.

Also, even if you're able to handle success, don't expect others to accept it without neurotic envy and jealousy pangs. Though *you* may not change, you can count on other people to alter their attitudes toward you. It's part of the price you pay for success. Don't be so naïve as to expect everyone to sit by passively and allow you to enjoy your newfound success. Often such unpleasantness will manifest itself in slander, which, as I discussed, stems from jealousy and self-contempt. The less someone's self-esteem, the more he is likely to resent your success. But it's nice to know that while there is nothing you can do to change the attitude of others toward you, you *can* choose to ignore them.

BREEDING GROUND FOR GUILT

It's nonsense to believe that your success causes others to suffer (unless they're neurotic, which is something over which you have no control), so you should be proud of your achievements. If you are fortunate enough to gain financial independence, don't allow others to prevent you from enjoying it.

It's irrational to think that just because there are people who live in poverty, you should feel guilty about your success. Unless someone else is poor because you robbed him, no poverty-stricken individual should be an obstacle to your happiness. On the contrary, as a result of your financial success, you will have made a great contribution to society, because you won't be a burden to the rest of the world. An added plus is that success puts you in a position to help people you deem to be in need if it is your desire to do so.

The worst cases of wealth-guilt complexes are often seen in people who have inherited, rather than earned, their fortunes. We've all seen enough of this sad phenomenon to suspect that such individuals often feel they don't deserve their wealth. If an individual suffers from this neurosis, the rational thing for him to do is use his wealth as a base for creating even more wealth rather than sit around and engage in self-flagellation.

In this vein, I recently read an alarming article about a group of wealthy, guilt-ridden heirs. In an effort to cleanse themselves of their self-imposed guilt, they had formed an organization for the purpose of figuring out "socially useful" ways to give away much of the wealth they had inherited. How sad that these confused individuals felt compelled to waste potentially productive, creative energy—not to mention capital—on such an unproductive project. Their mistake was to allow neurotic societal misfits and have-nots to saddle them with guilt feelings for something they not only were not responsible for, but which was not harming anyone else.

WHO SHALL RULE?

If you don't allow people to get to you via jealousy or guilt ploys, the only thing that can stop you from enjoying your financial success is you. Your attitude toward money is critical to your happiness. Either you control your money or it will control you. There are two diametrically opposed ways in which money can gain the upper hand on you.

The first is if you let money burn a hole in your pocket. If you've never possessed serious money before, it's very easy to get carried away with spending it. If your leap over the Financial Hurdle has been difficult, it's quite natural to want to enjoy your newly created wealth to the fullest extent possible. A little restraint, however, is in order. Don't enjoy your wealth so much and so fast that you wake up one morning only to find yourself back at square one.

A far more rational approach to handling prosperity is summarized in the **Touchies/No-Touchies Theory**, which states: *The wise individual accumulates two piles of chips—one labeled "touchies" and one labeled "no-touchies." The touchies are the chips you use to enjoy life—houses, cars, vacations, and other material possessions. The no-touchies are an insurance policy that gives you the security of knowing that if you happen to make a few bad decisions, or Old Man Murphy rains extra hard on your parade, you won't be faced with the challenge of having to start from scratch again.*

Just as important, money also can control you by making you overly fearful of losing it. Almost as bad as living beyond your means is living *beneath* your means. When you do so, money becomes an end in itself. Money can buy possessions and labor that not only make your life more comfortable, but can directly and indirectly give you the ultimate reward for crossing the Financial—freedom.

What good is money if you still have to perform tasks you dislike, tasks that you easily could afford to pay others to do for you? If you're so afraid of losing your money that it's a traumatic experience every time you need to come up with a few dollars to pay for something you want, you haven't really gained your freedom. Rather, you've only succeeded in imprisoning yourself. Put another way, if you allow money to rule you rather than the other way around, you're out of control—which means you are not in a position to make rational decisions.

THE MOST FICKLE FRIEND

How sweet it is at the top—the luxuries, the applause, the attention. Unfortunately, it's at the precise moment when you're enjoying it most that you're in the greatest danger of losing it all—so fast that it's hard, from your lofty vantage point, to even imagine. Never become so focused on enjoying your success that delude yourself into believing you're infallible. You can be certain competitors are plotting, Murphy's ghost is lying in wait, and the government is once again planning to change the rules of the game. Above all, recognize that circumstances will continually change, and if you aren't ready for such change, you're likely to get blindsided.

In reminding myself how quickly fame can slip away, I often think of David Seabury's likening life to a game of chess, warning that "Fate sits on the other side of the table watching your moves. . . . Make your moves according to the shifts of fortune, play by play."

The principles in this chapter have always worked for me. It's only when I've become careless and failed to follow my own rules that I have found myself once again heading in the wrong direction.

6 The People Hurdle

Human beings can be the source of so many of life's problems that it's essential to learn the art of dealing effectively with all makes and models in the People Store. There are five human realities, in particular, that one needs to understand and effectively deal with in order to clear the People Hurdle.

HUMAN REALITY NO. 1: IMPERFECTION

It's back to *is's* versus *ought to's*. Another human being is not what you think he ought to be; he is what he is. Deluding oneself about a person's true nature is not only self-deceitful, but self-destructive as well. First and foremost, human beings are imperfect. The failure to come to grips with this reality can be the source of endless frustration and disappointment. We want so badly for people to be perfect that we often hurt ourselves by expecting too much of them.

Once you accept the reality of man's imperfection, it's much easier to understand that the issue is not whether or not people will hurt you; rather, it's a matter of whether or not you *allow* them to hurt you. This hurt is often the result not only of your inability to cope with someone's imperfection, but of taking it upon yourself to try change a person into something he's not. If you insist on engaging in such a presumptuous task, you are guaranteed to experience the futility that comes with trying to overcome the impossible.

This futility is especially evident in dealing with those closest to you. Friends, spouses, parents, and children are people, too. As such, they are subject to the same human imperfections as everyone else. However, because of their close proximity to you, they are in a position to cause you much more pain than others—*if* you allow them to. By accepting the imperfection of people in our life, you dramatically reduce their ability to disappoint and hurt you.

HUMAN REALITY NO. 2: SELF-INTEREST

Through years of experience, I have come to the conclusion that all disagreements regarding the subject of self-interest versus altruism are not really disagreements at all. Rather, they are a matter of semantics. If you help an old lady to cross the street, you do so because it makes you feel good. The Absolute Moralist, however, insists that he performs the same deed out of sheer altruism. Alas, he deludes himself. The fact is that your action and his are one and the same. It is only the words (semantics) used to describe your actions that are different.

When the Absolute Moralist says that he helped an old lady cross the street, can he seriously deny that it made him feel good? I suppose he could split hairs and say that his good feeling was only a *result* of doing an altruistic deed, while your good feeling was the *intent* of your good deed. But let's examine that argument more closely.

First of all, the old lady doesn't give a hoot why either of you helped her; she's just happy to get to the other side of the street.

"Knock off the altruism speech, fuzz ball, and just get me across the street."

Second, what's wrong with doing a good deed for the reason that it makes you feel good? Did Mother Teresa do her admirable humanitarian work because it made her feel *bad*?

Third, if the Absolute Moralist really was thinking in altruistic terms, it wouldn't be so important to him to try to convince others that his good feeling came about only as an unintended side benefit.

Fourth, his good feeling was *not* an unintended benefit. Whether or not he consciously thought about it, he would not have helped the old lady cross the street if he didn't feel good about doing it.

Methinks what the Absolute Moralist in this case really needs is a good shrink to delve into his childhood problems and comb out his obviously tangled neurons. The fact that there are so many defective neurons in today's world is why I decided I could not, in good conscience, avoid the issue of self-interest versus altruism.

Few words have a more negative connotation than the term *self-interest*. When I was a kid, four-letter words were the ones you uttered secretly behind your parents' backs, but *self-interest* was a term you dared not even think about. Early on, you learned to hiss and boo anyone who proclaimed self-interest as a virtue.

Why has self-interest always been such a taboo subject? What is it about the reality of self-interest that sends so many people into a state of near hysteria? I believe the reason self-interest gets such a bad rap is that it is a threat to those who would like you to continue acting in *their* best interests instead of your own. *Rational* self-interest is not a problem; i.e., self-interest that does not involve forcible interference in the lives of others harms no one. The problem is the *irrational* self-interest of those who do not want you to act in your own best interest, who want to interfere in your life by pressuring you into doing what makes *them* happy.

No matter how vehemently some people may protest to the contrary, the reality is that self-interest is genetically programmed into every human being. You have no choice in the matter. However, if you are rational about self-interest, you *chiefly* regard your own interests, but not *solely*. Common sense tells you that you must regard the interests of others—especially loved ones and friends—in order to lead a fulfilling life.

Fellow human beings represent potential values to you, both in business and personal relationships. In order to harvest those values, you must add value to the lives of others. For this reason, the individual who practices rational self-interest is also a giving person, because he understands the soundness of mutually beneficial relationships.

On the other hand, when someone who is perceived to be altruistic does something for you, you're not likely to be impressed. Why? Because if he "gives" to everyone—even people he does not admire or respect—it has a diluting effect on the value of his gifts. I'm wary of gifts from supposedly altruistic people, because I don't like being in the dark about what the eventual payment might be—especially if it involves compound interest over a long period of time, which all too often is the case. I am not anxious to accumulate a lot of unspoken accounts payable. When, at some future date, the so-called altruistic person taps me on the shoulder and lets me know, perhaps in a subtle way, that the due date has arrived, my concern is that I may not be in a position to pay the debt.

Don't deceive yourself on this one. Recognize the reality that gifts from the professed altruistic almost always have hidden price tags, and they are usually greater than what you would have been willing to pay had the price been made clear from the outset. On the other hand, when you receive a gift from a person who practices rational self-interest, it is evidence of the value he places on his relationship with you.

The self-interest issue makes it clear why looking out for number one requires conscious, rational effort. Subconsciously, of course, you always make decisions that you believe are in your best interest, but there are times when you may delude yourself. Nevertheless, the fact that you are the one making the decisions guarantees that you are at least attempting to act in your own best interest. Hard as it is for many people to understand, even so called saints make decisions which they believe will make them happy. Take Mahatma Gandhi, the world-famous Indian ascetic who peacefully crusaded, primarily through fasting, for India's independence. Do I really believe Mahatma Gandhi acted in his own self-interest when he fasted almost to the point of starvation for the people of India? It's much stronger than just a belief. It is a DNA certainty!

Noble as his actions may have been, Gandhi was still a human being, and the actions of *all* human beings are chosen from the alternatives available to them at any given time. Whatever Mahatma Gandhi did, whether it was out of rational or irrational choice, it was because *he* chose to do it. If he acted in the hopes that he would bring happiness to others, then that was the method he chose to seek his *own* happiness. As with the Mother Teresa example mentioned earlier, Gandhi didn't lead a nonviolent movement to gain India's independence from the British Empire because he thought it would make him *unhappy*. It is only the means people choose to achieve their happiness that differ. In the case of Mahatma Gandhi, his methods for seeking personal gratification achieved results that were enormously beneficial for millions of his fellow countrymen.

While most of us would agree that Mahatma Gandhi and Mother Teresa were noble people, the same cannot be said of most martyrs. There is a fine line between someone who rationally seeks happiness by helping others and someone who seeks happiness for the sole reason of being a martyr. The latter is an irrationally selfish person with an enormous ego—an ego that must be continually fed adulation. It's wise to be wary of a martyr's supposedly selfless acts.

In most cases, of course, we don't consciously think about our actions toward loved ones. Even when you punish a child for inappropriate behavior, though you may feel badly about it, you believe you would feel even worse if you allowed him to get away with something that would be harmful to him either now or in the future.

In summation, it's important to recognize that there is no such thing as altruism in the true sense of the word, which is extremely difficult for Mr. Magoos and Ostriches to accept. There is only *rational* and *irrational* self-interest. If by *altruism* a person means that he is literally sacrificing himself for others, then what he is really talking about is nothing more than irrational self-interest—mistakenly doing what he believes will make him happy by surrendering a higher value to a lower value. Be wary of those who sincerely believe that their actions are altruistic, for they are far more vain and dangerous than those who only fake altruism (e.g., politicians and Hollywood types) in an effort to gain popularity. Such people have the capacity to do serious damage to those around them.

Thus, self-interest is neither bad nor good. It is simply a reality of human nature. But when you engage in *irrational* acts of self-interest, you are likely to hurt yourself and others. By contrast, when you engage in *rational* acts of self-interest, not only are you likely to experience more pleasure and less pain, your actions will often benefit others. Therefore, doing what is in your best interest and doing what is in the best interests of others are not mutually exclusive objectives.

From this day forward, resolve never again to cringe at the term *self-interest* and, instead, accept it as a reality of the human psyche.

HUMAN REALITY NO. 3: THE DEFINITION GAME

People love to play games, and one of their favorites is the Definition Game. The **Definition-Game Theory** states: *Every word, every act, every situation in life is defined by each individual subjectively, usually in such a way as to fit in comfortably with his own actions and/or the circumstances of the moment.*

Whether or not we realize it, we are all participants in the Definition Game. Because each of us is a unique human being with varying desires, tastes, prejudices, experiences, and personality traits, we see things through our own mental paradigms. Which is why it's prudent to assume that everyone, consciously or unconsciously, uses a definition guide that looks something like this:

Good is what I do; bad is what you do.
Right is what I do; wrong is what you do.
Honest is what I do; dishonest is what you do.
Fair is what I do; unfair is what you do.
Moral is what I do; immoral is what you do.
Ethical is what I do; unethical is what you do.

And on and on the game goes. If you have a realistic insight into how the Definition Game is played, you will be far less likely to assume that others are in tune with you when you think you are having a perfectly harmonious discussion.

The story of life overflows with tales of people nodding their heads in agreement, shaking hands, then facing each other in a courtroom at some future date. No doubt there were many occasions in pre-historic times when two Neanderthal men grunted affirmatively and walked away satisfied that they had agreed on some important point, only to end up trying to club each other to death a short time later when they realized they had misunderstood each other's grunts. The two big advantages they had over us were that there were no attorneys around to make matters worse and they didn't have to wait two or three years for their cases to come to court.

What further complicates the Definition Game is that people have a habit of changing their definitions as they go along. This is usually the result of one's established definitions being incompatible with his current actions. An Absolute Moralist, in particular, in his unceasing efforts to convert you to his beliefs, plays the Definition Game with an unmatched fervor. If only he can succeed in intimidating you into accepting his definitions, he will have laid the groundwork for getting you to act in his best interest rather than your own.

Another way of looking at the Definition Game is to be found in the **Victimizer-Victim Theory**, which states: *The victim is always you; the victimizer is always the other guy.* In other words, victimizing is something the other person does to you; it's never what you do to him.

Why is being a victim such an attractive label to so many people? Because by seeing himself as a victim, a person is able to justify just about any kind of immoral action. It is this human defect that pro-vides the populist fuel for mischievous politicians who shamelessly insist that their actions are for the benefit of the "middle class."

The dictionary only makes matters worse, because most words have many definitions, which in turn only encourages people to customize the definition of words to their liking. The problem with using the dictionary definition of a word is that you also have to look up the definitions of the words that are used to define that word. If you try this a few times, I think you'll arrive at the conclu-sion that the dictionary, in effect, leaves the real-world definition up to each individual.

Take a favorite Definition-Game word such as *right*. One dictionary I looked at defines it as follows:

> *Right*: "in accordance with what is *just* or good."
>
> *Just*: "in accordance with what is *right*."

Immediately, you reach an impasse. *Right* is in accordance with what is just, and *just* is in accordance with what is right. So, in effect, Webster has said to us, "You guys work it out. I don't want to get involved." Which is precisely why each individual defines words in accordance with what *he* wants them to mean. What's *your* definition of *right*? Is it the same as you neighbor's?

The same is true of honesty. When you say that someone is dishonest, what you really mean is that you and he differ on the definition of honesty, because he most likely believes that *you* are dishonest. That's why it's so important that your moral standards fit *your* guidelines for morality rather than someone else's. Never allow another person to be so presumptuous as to tell you what your moral code should be.

HUMAN REALITY NO. 4: THE LINE-DRAWING GAME

The **Line-Drawing-Game Theory** states: *Every individual subjec-tively draws his own lines with regard to right and wrong, based either*

on his moral standards, the moral standards of some person or group, or
moral standards that are convenient for him at any given time.

The Line-Drawing Game is something of a corollary of the
Definition Game. Not only do people define words to justify
their actions, they also define words *by* their actions. As with
the Definition Game, every human being is a participant in the
Line-Drawing Game, whether or not he is conscious of it. Through
a person's actions and inactions, he advertises to the world on which
side of which lines he stands. Whether or not we are consciously
aware of it, we draw our lines where they are needed to justify our
own behavior and our own particular set of circumstances.

For example, when a person steals groceries because he believes
he has a "right" to eat, his actions clearly reveal his definition of
the word *right*. When a homicide bomber kills innocent civilians,
he undoubtedly believes that his actions are based on sound moral
principles. His misguided, maniacal actions speak worlds about his
definition of the word *moral*.

Every individual arbitrarily draws his lines between right and
wrong, carefully placing those lines in such a way as to be certain
that his actions will always lie on the side of right. Where another
individual draws his lines may seem immoral to you, but such an
individual is unlikely to be interested in your opinion of right and
wrong. He may, however, see your opinions as a justifiable cause to
declare war on you.

Problems begin to set in when Absolute Moralists decide to
start drawing lines for people other than themselves. Since billions
of individuals can never agree on all things at all times, a statement
such as "someone has to draw the line somewhere" is a euphemism
for "do it my way." No one has the knowledge, let alone the moral
authority, to be a line drawer for others.

Unfortunately, there has never been a scarcity of crusaders,
bureaucrats, and would-be dictators willing to step forward and
draw lines for their fellow citizens. And since it is impossible for
every member of a society to simultaneously agree on anything—
let alone *everything*—any line drawn by others, whether under

the guise of a commandment, law, or dictum, is destined to make many people unhappy.

Property rights constitute an area where real, physical lines are drawn. How far back should we go to determine who originally occupied an area of land? Every government in control of an area of land today draws a line that assures that its ownership is valid. It is not about to lend credence to the reality that the land it now occupies was taken from some other group of people decades, hundreds, or even thousands of years earlier. When it comes to matters of land ownership, *current* possession is, indeed, nine-tenths of the law.

That is what makes the so-called Israeli-occupation argument such a red herring. Even if the Palestinians had "owned" the land now occupied by the Israelis (which they did not), it wouldn't matter. When a large part of the Arab world again attacked Israel in 1967, openly stating that its objective was to push all Israelis into the sea, Israel crushed its attackers and, as any rational person would have expected, took some Arab land in the process. Welcome to the world of reality. As I said, every piece of land on the globe is now controlled by a government that took it, by force, from someone else. The most important point Arabs made with their 1967 attack on Israel was that if you don't want your land to be taken from you, an excellent way to avoid such a fate is to not attempt to annihilate another nation.

Court fights over rightful land titles are common, with title companies employed to trace ownership back to the original owners. The only problem with title searches is that they go back only to the point where the line was arbitrarily drawn by the most recent conquerors of a given geographic area. All discussions of property rights begin with the premise that the original owner of a given piece of land was the first owner *after* it was taken by force from some other group of people. Understandably, American Indians, New Zealand Maoris, and Australian Aborigines don't give much validity to title searches.

As with the Definition Game, what considerably complicates the matter is that, in addition to the fact that everyone draws his lines subjectively, people also are constantly erasing old lines and drawing new ones to conform to changing circumstances. One of the reasons this occurs so frequently is that a majority of people do not take the trouble to analyze the moral standards by which they want to live their lives. As a result, whenever they happen to want something that is on the wrong side of one of their lines, they simply relocate that line so it falls on their side of the line. Such line-drawing tactics are commonly referred to as *situational ethics*.

Never allow yourself to be intimidated by the line-drawing decisions of others. Make it clear to those who would intimidate you into agreeing with them that you require no help in deciding where to place your lines. By the same token, where others wish to draw their lines is their business, so long as those lines do not infringe on your freedom. Though we have no choice when it comes to government laws and decrees, it *is* within our power to resist the urge to draw lines for others.

HUMAN REALITY NO. 5: IRRATIONALITY

Irrational is the opposite of *rational,* the latter referring to words and actions based on logic and reason. Unfortunately, all human beings are irrational at least some of the time, but occasional irrationality is not a major problem. People problems arise from those who are *excessively* and *consistently* irrational. To clear the People Hurdle, you have to become adept at spotting irrationality in others and, just as important, at monitoring and controlling your thought processes to assure that your own words and actions are rational.

Since each individual's definition of reason and logic may vary, how can you be certain whose perception of rationality is correct? From a long-term perspective, the answer is simple: The irrational person will usually fail to achieve his objectives, while the rational person will usually succeed.

As a simple guideline for making rational decisions, you should develop the habit of asking yourself two questions. First, does my proposed action have the potential to better my existence, either by bringing me more pleasure or less pain? Second, will my action in any way infringe on anyone else's natural rights?

Remember, to take action that is happiness oriented, you have to be aware of what you're doing and why you're doing it. And to accomplish that, you must possess an accurate perception of reality—the very foundation of looking out for number one. If the actions a person takes to enrich his life are contrary to the facts, then such actions are irrational. Whether he acts in opposition to reality because of a malfunction of his reasoning powers or because he deceives himself is irrelevant. In either case, he is destined to suffer bad consequences over the long term.

In *Atlas Shrugged*, John Galt explains why irrationality automatically negates the possibility of happiness when he states, "Happiness is possible only to a rational man, the man who desires nothing but rational goals, seeks nothing but rational values and finds his joy in nothing but rational actions."

Facts can best be ascertained when your intellect, rather than your emotions, is in control. During periods of relaxed solitude, when there is nothing to distract your thoughts, you should think about the philosophical issues that most affect your life. Then have enough confidence in your analysis to remain loyal to your predetermined code of behavior when inevitable encounters with irrational people occur. Make a written-in-stone commitment, well in advance, not to allow your emotions to sway you in your time of need.

One word of caution: Just because you act rationally, don't assume that everyone around will do likewise. They won't. The path to a happy life is obstructed by irrational people who are ready, willing, and able to scramble your grey matter if you aren't properly equipped to deal with them.

SPOTTING AN IRRATIONAL ARGUMENT

How do you know when someone is being irrational? First, you have to learn to see past a person's words to his premise, because you may find that you don't agree with that premise. For example, if an interviewer asks me a question such as, "You aren't really interested in helping others, are you?" I have no way of responding to such a question without asking the interviewer to first define his words. If by *others* he is alluding to *all* people, then my answer is *no*. There are terrorists, child molesters, and Absolute Moralists whom I do not wish to help in any way. Yet I have very deep feelings for many people, primarily those individuals who add value to my life, and I am always interested in helping such people.

The same is true of the word *helping*. If by *helping* the questioner means giving others something for nothing, again my answer is *no*. I am, however, more than happy to help if it means doing something for an individual with whom I have a valuable relationship. I have no desire to distribute love, friendship, money, or any other valuable commodity indiscriminately to anyone who happens to cross my path. To do so would lessen the value of what I have to offer people whom I genuinely care about, such as friends, family, and business associates. Neither do I wish to receive love, friendship, money, or anything else of value from anyone who has not received, or does not expect to receive, something of value from me.

Never feel obliged to answer a question until the asker defines his terms. If you find that a question is based on what you consider to be a false premise, then *any* answer you give will be dishonest. I often find that when I unmask the premise, no meaningful question exists; rather, it becomes a hypothetical question. A meaningful question deals with reality; a hypothetical question is a forced illusion. I don't have time to clutter my mind with hypothetical questions based on false premises.

The illogical person tips his hand in many other ways, but you have to be alert to pick up on the signs. Irrational people stray from the main point; they dwell on the irrelevant; they rely on nonfactual slogans; they generalize; they use invalid analogies; and they are masters at "proving" a point by simply restating it as a fact, a technique commonly referred to as an *a priori* argument. Regardless of the tactic employed, the objective is similar to that of a magician, politician, or criminal-defense attorney: Distract the person's attention from the real issue.

Perhaps the most common behavioral pattern of the irrational person is emotional excess. Whenever I feel strongly about making a point, I remind myself of the telltale observation by Queen Gertrude in Shakespeare's *Hamlet*, "The lady doth protest too much, methinks." The more one belabors a point, the more skeptical I become; the louder one talks, the more I back off. Indignation raises doubts in the minds of those to whom you wish to make your point. Again, the power of the understatement is enormous. Say it once; say it calmly; say it firmly. If your point is rational, state it in a rational manner. Every statement beyond that is counterproductive.

What I am referring to here is the **Protesting-Lady Theory**, which states: *The more someone dwells on a point, the more likely it is that the opposite is true.*

If you pay close attention to the remarkable consistency of this principle, your friends will think you're clairvoyant. Following are a few examples of how you might employ the principle underlying the Protesting-Lady Theory in everyday life.

Statement: I've got it all together now.

Translation: I'm so screwed up that I'm past the point of even acknowledging it.

Statement: My wife and I never argue. We're more in love today than when we were newlyweds. We have the perfect marriage.

Translation: My marriage is a bore, my wife and I hardly speak, and I'm just waiting for the right time to file for divorce.

Statement: I'm making money hand over fist—pay cash for everything. Got it made.

Translation: I'm one step ahead of the sheriff, my Mercedes is on a month-to-month lease, and unless a miracle happens, I'll be belly-up within a month.

Beware of the person who overstates his case. He's sending you a message, but you have to be alert to hear it. And should you ever find *yourself* trying too hard to impress a listener, best you reexamine the facts—as well as your motives—because there's a good chance you may be acting irrationally.

CLEARING THE WEEDS

To the extent you allow weeds to grow and remain in your life's garden, you are asking for a great deal of unnecessary frustration and turmoil. The weeds that grow most out of control are known as *neurotics*, i.e., people with emotional disorders. Actually, each of us is a little neurotic in one area or another, at least on some occasions. But it's those people who have either too many neuroses or a specific neurosis that is extreme who have the potential to seriously disrupt your life. Eliminating people problems requires that you become skilled at spotting neurotic traits in those around you and developing the self-discipline to ignore those who are severely afflicted.

Fortunately, you have a weapon at your disposal that gives you the capacity to remove most of the people weeds from your life. The weapon I am referring to is encompassed in the **Anti-Neurotic Theory**, which states: *Ignore all irrational remarks and actions of normal people and all remarks and actions—irrational or otherwise—of neurotic people.*

Have you ever had a person say or do something to you that was so outrageous it made you feel like picking up the telephone and describing the details to everyone you know? Have you every been so frustrated by someone's neurotic actions that you felt like roaming the streets and explaining it to anyone and everyone who will stop and listen to you?

Such a reaction is known as: Big Mistake. If what a person said or did was so outrageous, that's reason enough not to waste your time explaining it to anyone. Why further aggravate yourself? Worse, if it's truly outrageous, others might even think you're exaggerating. The most rational way to handle such a situation is to simply ignore it. When your instinct is to rant and rave about a grave injustice that has been done to you, granted it's very difficult to keep your mouth shut and blank the matter out of your mind. Nevertheless, the painful self-discipline required to do so is well worth the price, because you will absolutely love yourself in the morning.

THE COMPROMISE

If a neurotic person refuses to be ignored, does that mean you're helpless? Is a compromise in order? No. If your objective is to make certain that a person will continue to act irrationally, you need only give in to his neurosis by compromising. When you compromise—even if it's only 1 percent—what you're really doing is giving in. If a person displays excessive neurotic behavior that is causing you persistent discomfort, you owe it to yourself, as well as to him, not to give him hope by allowing your relationship to drag on.

The problem with compromising is that it encourages irrationality, and that in turn prolongs the inevitable moment when you will be forced to face up to the reality that the relationship must end. And, like all problems whose permanent solutions are postponed, when that inevitable moment finally arrives, it will be that much more difficult to close the door. That's because the passage of time will have given the neurotic individual the illusion that you've resolved your differences.

THE DEBATE

Another common mistake people make with neurotics is to engage in ongoing discussions in an attempt to reach an agreement on who is in the right. Discussion in itself is not a bad thing, *provided* the individual with whom you are having the discussion is rational. But when a discussion reaches an impasse, or the other person becomes irrational, you begin to enter the dangerous area of "The Debate"—a classic exercise in futility. When The Debate enters the picture, it's your cue to exit.

In using the word *discussion*, I'm referring to a calm, rational, analysis of the facts. By *debate*, I'm referring to an *irrational* exchange of words in which at least one party either clings to a false premise, talks in a loud and/or harsh tone as though he believes he can somehow drown out the facts, or employs meaningless slogans, broad-sweeping statements, or slanderous words as some sort of proof that he is right. Debating gives hope to the wounded neurotic, because he believes all things are possible via this verbal spider web. The Debate is a miraculous channel through which an illusion can be created that logic and reason do not exist.

The professional debater can dangle an irresistible carrot under your nose. He is accomplished at saying things that are so illogical that it's difficult to avoid the temptation to prove him wrong. If you take his bait and answer a question based on a false premise, it becomes a kind of implied consent in his mind, which only encourages him to raise the verbal stakes. Since he has no intention of using logic in his argument, he can easily escape your reasoning trap by jumping from one ill-founded premise to another.

It takes a lot of self-discipline to ignore those who would entice you into a debate, but the first time you succeed in turning your back on a neurotic debater, you'll experience a wonderful feeling of self-respect. Such self-respect is derived from the knowledge that you are above dignifying irrational chatter. But to accomplish this, you must dare to precipitate a crisis. You have to have the courage to confront the neurotic, in a civil but straightforward manner, and make your desire to opt out of your relationship with him crystal clear. And should he become nasty about it, don't make the mistake of reciprocating. State your case in a calm, civilized, firm manner, being as pleasant as circumstances will allow. Then excuse yourself and head for the nearest exit.

Talking, arguing, or even begging does not work with an irrational person, and attempting to persuade him through logical argument will only frustrate you. If he's clever, you will often find yourself boxed into being "damned if you do and damned if you don't." In short, dealing with an irrational person is a can't-win proposition.

"Hee, hee . . . 2 + 2 equals 5 . . . yuk, yuk, yuk . . ."

You know you're in a can't-win situation when anything you say, no matter how well intended, only ups the debating ante.

If someone constantly surrounds you on all sides with irrational arguments, it's a signal that it's time for you to take control of your life. Do whatever is necessary to remove yourself from his presence, but do remove yourself. The most certain way to create enemies is to allow neurotic people to remain in your life.

If, instead, you choose to ignore a neurotic individual, he may pout for a while, but the odds are that he will eventually go away and bother someone else who is more disposed to do battle with him. A neurotic person would much prefer to devote his energies to someone who is willing to vigorously argue with him. Ignoring isn't a matter of just refusing to acknowledge the individual who is trying to harass you. It means *totally* ignoring him, which in turn means totally ignoring *all* of his words and actions.

Continual contact with a neurotic individual can lead to second-guessing yourself. Figuratively speaking, an accomplished neurotic can make you believe that day is night and that two plus two equals five. Can you imagine a worse nightmare than rattling the bars of your cage and having peanuts being tossed to you by a neurotic individual whom you carelessly allowed to remain in your life?

Being involved with a neurotic person puts you in danger of becoming a victim of the **I'm-Crazy, You're-Sane Theory**, which states: *If you allow a neurotic individual to remain in your life, you run the risk of his convincing you that he is perfectly sane and that you're the one who's crazy.*

EXIT, STAGE RIGHT

Humoring—which includes compromising—is the equivalent of taking an aspirin for a headache. But when you completely eliminate a neurotic from your life, you are effecting a permanent cure. The neurotic not only will leave you alone, but in all likelihood he'll forget about you. It's only when you allow him to remain in your life and try to help him "see the light" through reason and logic that you remain at the forefront of his mind.

In cases where a neurotic individual persists even after you have shown him a complete lack of attention, you must be strong enough to take swift and firm action to make it clear that you wish to terminate your relationship with him. This may sound harsh, but you have no moral obligation to deal with irrational people. You need not accept unpleasantness for the sake of keeping the peace. You have a right to live your life as you please, so long as you are not harming anyone else.

It's also a serious mistake to attempt to change a neurotic person. Like you, the neurotic has a right to live his life as he pleases, without interference from others. That, however, does not mean his cause is hopeless. It's always possible that he may get well on his own, and—who knows?—at some future point in time he could become a rose in your life's garden. But until and unless such an unlikely transformation occurs, you should make it a point to steer clear of him. By doing so, you will save yourself a considerable amount of aggravation and, at the same time, spare the neurotic a crutch that will only worsen his neurosis.

Remember: *People will bother you until you no longer allow them to.* Those who consistently exasperate you should be eliminated from your life, while those who display rational, positive qualities should be looked upon as welcome additions. Decide how *you* want to live your life, then proceed accordingly as though there were no irrational people around to bother you. If you allow neurotic individuals to have an effect on your decisions, you'll be out of control, which is a condition that is not in harmony with looking out for number one.

You're on your way to clearing the People Hurdle when you become proficient at redirecting the energy you once used for hassling with neurotic people to finding ways to attract rational people who can add value to your life.

7 The Friendship Hurdle

While the previous chapter focused on how to prevent people from causing you pain, the Friendship Hurdle is about how to find and form relationships with people who can add value to your life. There are more than seven billion human beings in the People Store, and you only need to find a handful of the right individuals to fill your companionship needs. Always keep in mind, however, that you will never find the roses unless you keep the weeds cut down to size.

COPING WITH LONELINESS

Survey after survey has pinpointed loneliness as one of the biggest problems that most people face. Nevertheless, I believe you have to conquer loneliness before you can excel at cultivating friendships.

In other words, the first step toward conquering loneliness is to learn to enjoy yourself.

No matter who you are, no matter what you've accomplished, and no matter how many friends you have, the reality is that you came into this world alone and, like it or not, you're going to go out the same way. Regardless of how close you are to another person, you will always be an entity unto yourself. No one can ever know all there is to know about you. No one can get inside your mind and effect a psychological merger of two separate beings. Someone can be an integral part of your life, but never a literal part of *you*. Once you understand and accept this reality, you will be much better equipped to put loneliness into proper perspective.

Given that you entered the world alone and will exit alone, it only makes good sense to get to know yourself as well as possible. Once you do, you will have a good understanding of what it means to be "never less alone than when alone." In simple terms, you can't enjoy other people until you learn to enjoy yourself. You can't fully appreciate the company of others if the fear of loneliness is foremost in your mind.

There's no reason that being alone should be a lonely experience. On the contrary, it can be an enriching experience, provided you like yourself. It would be appropriate to say that it's a matter of becoming friends with Number One. Perhaps the best way to look at it is to ask yourself, "If I can't enjoy my own company, why should I expect anyone else to enjoy it?" Learn to appreciate solitude for what it is—an opportunity to engage in activities that cannot be as fulfilling when you're in the presence of others. "I never found the companion," said Thoreau, "that was so companionable as solitude."

Reading, for example, is one of the most delightful experiences life has to offer, a habit you would do well to cultivate if its treasures have escaped you. Obviously, reading is an activity that is more enjoyable when there is no one around to distract you. Along with the pleasure it brings, reading also broadens your horizons, which in turn makes you a more interesting person.

Meditation is another activity that is rewarding when experienced alone. It not only relaxes you, but it can also be a catalyst for bringing forth solutions to problems that you may have trouble handling when others are around. As a bonus, your value to others increases when your mind is cleansed of mental cobwebs.

Again, aloneness and loneliness are two distinct mental states. If you keep aloneness in proper perspective—if you see it as an opportunity to experience some of life's greatest pleasures—you will be able to eliminate the word *loneliness* from your vocabulary. If you use moments of solitude intelligently rather than allowing them to foment unfounded fears of loneliness, you will find yourself getting much more enjoyment out of the time you spend with others.

Those who have difficulty grasping this principle often go to embarrassing lengths to conquer loneliness through overkill, surrounding themselves with far too many people far too much of the time. The solution to loneliness isn't to flood your life with every make and model in the People Store. Some of the loneliest moments of my life have been spent in large crowds.

What's far more important than striving to have a lot of people around you is having friendships that are based on mutual admiration and respect. If you enjoy just one such relationship, you should consider yourself fortunate. It's a matter of quality over quantity. A person can have many acquaintances, yet still be very lonely.

All too often, people are more than willing to compromise their integrity in a desperate effort to avoid loneliness. Some, for example, seek to attract "hangers-on." One doesn't need to be a celebrity to be surrounded by hangers-on; leeches are readily available to anyone. Another way of compromising your integrity is to conform to the lifestyle of others in an effort to gain acceptance, which often results in forsaking your moral principles in the process. Sadly, this mistake always backfires, because the person doing the conforming decreases the chances of finding people with whom he has the most in common. The desire to be "one of the guys" is a nice objective for high schoolers, but it doesn't play well in the adult world.

BUILDING BLOCKS

Rational self-interest provides the basis for the essential component of mutually beneficial relationships. Those who have difficulty making and keeping friends usually are afflicted with the same virus that stems from the World-Owes-Me-a-Living Theory. No one owes you, or anyone else, anything, so don't make the mistake of seeking an unearned friendship. If you learn to deal with people on a value-added basis, you will be amazed at how willingly they in turn will fill your needs (assuming that they, too, understand the efficacy of value-for-value relationships).

When you do something for a friend, it should be a conscious, rational decision on your part—a goodwill gesture toward another person whose friendship represents a value to you. It's not a complicated proposition. The only caveat is that you must be certain you are feeding your Weight-and-Balance Happiness Scale correct information at all times. Meaningful relationships are based on rational self-interest. When two people clearly understand this principle, it lays the best possible foundation for a healthy, long-lasting relationship.

The dictionary defines the word *true* (in the friendship sense) as "loyal, faithful, and sincere." If one accepts this definition, then certainly there is such a thing as a true friend. There are people you can count on to be loyal, faithful, and sincere. They are the people who have concluded, through personal experience, that what they receive from their relationship with you is worth their effort to be loyal, faithful, and sincere. In most cases, of course, such conclusions are subconscious.

One of the best barometers of friendship is how friends react when they hear unfavorable, even slanderous, things about you. Verbal assaults on you should have little or no effect on true friends. Anyone who knows you well enough to call you a friend, yet gives weight to the negative comments of others, is telling you something about his own character and the value he places on your friendship. If secondhand remarks override his firsthand experience with you, he's doing you a favor by eliminating himself from your life. After all, had such a "friend" not shown his true colors, his lack of character might have surfaced during a crisis, when the consequences of his lack of loyalty could have been far more damaging to you.

Personally, I make an effort not only to completely disregard unfavorable remarks about friends, but I pretty much discount anything negative I hear about *anyone*. I do this out of rational self-interest, because experience has taught me that all too often I end up admiring a person about whom I have heard defamatory remarks.

THE PRICE OF FRIENDSHIP

Remember, everything worthwhile has a price. The price of friendship varies in amount and form, but, make no mistake about it, there is always a payment involved. The payment may require your investing a certain number of hours per week in conversation, it may mean that you are counted on for continual inspiration, or it may translate into your having to forego a facet of your life that is important to you. Whatever it may be, just be aware that there *is* a payment.

Every person in the Free-Enterprise Friendship Market has needs. When you fill one or more of those needs for someone, you are, in effect, "paying" for his friendship. It's when you aren't willing to pay for someone's friendship—i.e., when you aren't prepared to fill a need of his—that you begin having problems with the Friendship Hurdle. To one extent or another, each of us possesses the self-destructive something-for-nothing urge, which always produces bad long-term results. To the degree you are successful in keeping this urge under control, your chances of making and keeping good friends are greatly enhanced. The less you delude yourself about the long-term cost of a friendship, the less likely it is that you will end up in unpleasant relationships.

Above all, be vigilant when it comes to advertising your true self. If you try to be something you're not, those people who have the most in common with you—presumably individuals who share similar values to yours—will not recognize you when you make your appearance. Worse, those whom you would prefer not to have in your life will often be the very ones most attracted to your disguise, which can result in dishonest and unpleasant relationships.

You should not become a different person just because you are in the presence of people who are not like you. The only way to survive socially over the long term is to be the real you at all times, consciously resisting the temptation to adjust your personality to more easily fit into each new social setting. Being what you believe others expect you to be rather than what you really are means you are not in control of your life. Trying to be all things to all people doesn't work, which is reason enough to consistently display yourself as you really are if your aim is to attract people who can add genuine value to your life.

RETENTION

The simplest way to destroy a good friendship is to forget that friends are people and that people are not perfect. They'll disappoint you, they'll hurt you, they'll let you down. Depending on the degree and frequency, this doesn't necessarily mean that a person isn't a good friend. It just reaffirms what you already know about human beings: They are not perfect. That being the case, if a friendship is worthwhile from your standpoint, the key to surviving disappointing actions on the part of your friend is forgiveness.

Also, keep in mind that something that disappoints and hurts you might look very different through the other person's eyes. Like all human beings, your friend plays the Definition and Line-Drawing Games. Though you may have strong convictions that you're in the right, his line drawing, as well as his definitions, will sometimes vary from yours. Of course, if it happens too often, you should probably reevaluate whether your values are compatible enough to sustain a healthy friendship with that person.

I seldom have flare-ups with friends anymore, because I make it a point to give them the benefit of the doubt. Whenever a friend does something that annoys me, I try to remember that people have been mad at me at times for reasons I felt were unjustified.

It therefore seems reasonable to assume that my friend's annoying actions probably weren't meant in a detrimental way.

There may be all kinds of extenuating circumstances that could cause a friend to act in a manner that irritates you. He might be having financial difficulties, he might not be getting along with his wife, or it's just possible that *you* might have done something that irritated *him*—which is why it's wise to give him the benefit of the doubt. It's not in your best interest to harbor grudges, particularly toward those from whom you derive pleasure.

Does this mean you should put up with any amount of unpleasantness a friend may cause you? Of course not. The degree to which you put up with unpleasantness should be reasonably proportionate to the value you place on the friendship. So long as what you derive from the friendship outweighs the cost, it makes perfect sense to forgive and forget. But when it's no longer worth the price, it's probably time to make your exit. Just make sure you don't depart impulsively in a moment of anger, when you are reacting emotionally to something you may see in a different light after you've had some time to think it through. One moment of anger can produce a lifetime of regret, particularly where friends are concerned.

FRIENDSHIP POISONS

I previously discussed some of the dangers inherent in an oversized ego when it comes to financial matters, and what I said goes for all areas of life. When it comes to friendships, when the ego stands too tall, relationships begin to fall. When that dinosaur gets up and steps on your house, just make sure that a valuable friendship isn't inside. If you can't afford to feed an overstuffed ego, you can be certain that your friends don't want to be saddled with the job. The cost of an insatiable ego can be a loss of friends as well as a danger to your financial well-being.

Another excellent way to reduce the quality and quantity of your friendships is to cultivate a reputation as the perpetual bearer of bad tidings. It's one thing to occasionally discuss problems with friends; it's another to overwhelm them with your troubles. The reality is that people, by and large, have an aversion to other people's problems because they have enough of their own. So it's quite natural for them to avoid the company of those who are continual bearers of negative messages.

If being perpetually negative doesn't do the trick, emotionally and/or psychologically disrobing yourself will. It's nice to have intimates you can confide in, but that doesn't mean you should make your every thought public. Television talk shows have made it popular for disturbed humanoids to share the most intimate parts of their lives with millions of strangers. Aside from making asses of themselves, they set a horrible example for already brain-dead audiences desperate for ever more outrageous forms of entertainment.

When there's nothing else for someone to discover about you, you lose your luster in that person's eyes. No one can climb inside your brain and become a literal part of you. Even if you have an extraordinarily close relationship with another person, you are still an individual entity, so you shouldn't feel as though you have a moral obligation to make every facet of your life an open book— not even to your closest friend. The majority of your most personal thoughts and feelings should remain your private property. As we all know, nature has a nasty habit of converting friends into enemies, and when that happens it's helpful if they're not carrying around a mental diary of your private life.

Perhaps the easiest way of all to destroy a friendship is to wake up one morning and realize that your accounts payable to someone has far outgrown your receivables. If a person is a good friend, it's easy to be presumptuous and take liberties you wouldn't think of taking with strangers. But does it make any sense to treat friends worse than strangers? Never lose sight of the fact that friends have Weight-and-Balance Happiness Scales, too. They can't afford to carry overdue receivables on their books indefinitely any more than you can. When you allow a friendship to become too one-sided— with your friend being the creditor and you the debtor—it moves out of the realm of a friendship and into an obligatory relationship.

Your friendship debts can become so great that you literally lose your freedom.

Finally, remember that the easiest thing in the world is to make commitments; the hardest is to keep them. Don't leave the word *yes* carelessly lying around on the tip of your tongue. Best you keep it safely tucked away, to be used only for special occasions. A good rule to remember: Learn to say no politely and pleasantly, but immediately and firmly.

That doesn't mean you should say no to everything a friend asks of you. Rather, it's a matter of not making promises you can't keep. It's that old struggle again between short-term patching and long-term solutions. A friend may love you in the short term for promising to do something for him, but later become angry with you for not following through on your commitment. Conversely, he may initially be irritated if you immediately refuse his request, but eventually he'll probably forget the incident or even respect you for having had the self-discipline not to make a commitment that you weren't prepared to keep. The latter is more likely to be the case if you tell him, right out front and in a rational manner, your reasons for having to refuse his request.

The problem becomes even more delicate when you've made a commitment, then realize that you either can't keep it or, for one reason or another, don't want to keep it. Generally speaking, I believe it's important to keep one's commitments. However, if it becomes apparent that you've made a mistake by committing to something, you certainly are under no moral obligation to follow through if, for example, you feel that what you've committed to is in conflict with your integrity or in some other way harmful to your reputation.

As an example, suppose, in a moment of anger, that you agree to help a friend carry out a vendetta against someone whom both of you dislike. When you come to your senses and realize that such an action is immoral, you certainly have a right to change your mind. In this illustration, *not* backing out of your commitment would be immoral.

In such a case, it's wise to abide by the principle of precipitating a crisis sooner rather than later. If you agree to do something, then later realize you've made a mistake, explain your position in a straightforward manner, but leave no doubt in the other person's mind that your decision not to go through with your commitment is final. If you wait until tomorrow to confront your friend, it will be that much harder, and the day after that will be even more difficult.

To avoid such an unpleasant circumstance, it's far better to catch yourself *before* making an impulsive commitment. There are many things you may wish to do for friends, but it's unrealistic to try to do all of them. Rid yourself of the illusion that you can be all things to all people. It makes good sense to choose only those things that you are best equipped to handle at any given time for those friends who are most important to you. You will never please everyone, so your focus should be on doing what *you* think is the right thing to do under the circumstances.

Overcommitting in a frantic effort to make or keep friends is a major mistake. All too often the result is that you end up being seen as the bad guy, while those who didn't offer to lift a finger to help are likely to get off scot-free. It's yet another example of the You-Won't-Get-Credit-for-It Theory, and one that has the potential to cause you a lot of frustration and pain.

THE RESPECT VIRUS

When it comes to maintaining friendships, respect is contagious. If you possess self-respect, it's likely you will have the respect of others as well. But if you lack self-respect, the opposite is most likely to be true. The easiest way to lack respect is to engage in an activity that is against your code of ethics. This commonly occurs when you try too hard to please others or attempt to avoid paying the full price for something.

Self-respect, which results from faithful adherence to one's beliefs, is a rare treasure. As would be expected of anything of value, the price of maintaining one's self-respect is considerable.

Part of the price comes in the form of self-discipline, which can make you unpopular in the short term. But over the long term, even those who may have chastised you for not going along with something you believed would compromise your integrity will end up respecting you (though not necessarily liking you) for remaining strong.

A simple rule to follow is: *Never compromise your integrity for anything or anybody.*

CONTRACTION

Also, recognize that a healthy social life is not about how many friends you accumulate; it's about the quality of your friendships. If you've accumulated a lot of excess baggage in the way of acquaintances who contribute more discomfort than pleasure to your life, by now you know you can't afford the extra baggage. I spoke earlier of the wisdom of precipitating a crisis sooner rather than later, and it's such an important point that I would like to reemphasize it here in the form of the **Crummy-Friendship Theory**, which states: *A crummy friendship is one in which you consistently give more than you receive.*

It's okay to give more than you receive for short periods of time, but after awhile it becomes a burden. If you've made the mistake of getting into a friendship that you now realize is going in the wrong direction, cut it off before it gets out of control. Just because you made an initial error in judgment does not mean you have an obligation to perpetuate the relationship and endure further suffering. When you try to smooth over irritating situations, they are only likely to get worse. The other person often misinterprets your nonresistance as encouragement, with the end result being bad feelings all the way around when the situation finally comes to a head.

As discussed in the People Hurdle chapter, you don't have to yield to everyone who has a desire to enter your private world. And if the wrong person does manage to slip in, it's up to you to take control of the situation. Don't leave the matter of friendship to the whims of others, and don't procrastinate. Take matters into your own hands *today*. Anyone who causes you problems or discomfort—be he a friend, relative, or, above all, an uninvited guest—is an aggressor on your happiness, and no one has a right to commit aggression against you.

It is certainly not cruel to exit a relationship that is causing you pain. On the contrary, it's a wise and rational action to do so. In fact, it's good for both you *and* the other party, because the long-term result of your failure to take action is likely to be a great deal of unpleasantness all around.

FOCUSING ON THE BASICS

If you haven't been successful in finding value-based friendships, there's a good chance you haven't been willing to give equal value for that which you hope to receive in return. The Weight-and-Balance Happiness Scales of others may be telling them to stay away.

The fact is that you *can* find mutually beneficial relationships if it's important enough to you to make the effort. It's amazing how many wonderful, value-oriented people there are in the People Store. Percentagewise, the figure may be small, but in absolute numbers there are more than enough to go around. The problem is that the roses are hiding among millions of weeds, so it's up to you to put forth the effort to uncover them.

The good thing is that you don't need hundreds of friends to make you happy. A few truly good friends can more than fill your needs. And your odds of finding just a few of the right kind people are very good, *provided* you are willing to expend the necessary effort.

"I have two neurotics and a weed in the car that I'd like to trade for a couple of roses."

8 The Love Hurdle

The dictionary partially defines love as "a profoundly tender, passionate affection for a another person." The operative word in this definition is *passionate*. In its purest form, the feeling of passionate affection is an inexplicable physical attraction—an indefinable chemistry—that finds its ultimate celebration in sexual expression. The physical-attraction aspect is important, because without it there would be no such thing as romantic love. You may love many things about a person, but if romantic affinity isn't present, all you really have is a friend. Physical attraction is what distinguishes between a love relationship and a friendship.

Physical attraction relies on beauty only insofar as one acknowledges that beauty is subjective. What you see when you look at the person you love can be quite different from what others see. The deep affection you may feel for someone is based on a total

162

package, including such things as physical appearance, intellectual capacity, and emotional makeup, and it is this total package to which you are physically attracted.

Love is not an either/or proposition; it is measured in degrees. If you feel romantic love for two people, the extent of love you feel for one person will exceed the love you feel for the other. Also, the *kind* of love you feel for one individual is different from that which you feel for another, because each person possesses unique characteristics. It is certainly possible to have deep, passionate feelings for more than one member of the opposite sex. Lacking control over such feelings, however, can lead to self-destructive behavior.

NEGATIVE SIGNALS

For many, the first step towards finding true love is to terminate a relationship where real love does not exist. There are endless signals that will tell you if you're in the wrong relationship, but you have to be alert to pick up on them. Even more important, you have to have the courage not only to acknowledge a negative signal, but to actually do something about it. A few of the more obvious of these signals are discussed below.

THE COMPROMISE SIGNAL

There is probably much truth to the old adage that opposites attract, but an even more important reality is that they usually don't stay together very long. And even if they do, it's not likely to be a happy relationship. Finding true love is difficult enough even when your tastes are similar to those of the other person, but common sense tells you that if two people don't enjoy many of the same things in life, the chances of long-term success in their relationship are dramatically reduced.

When it comes to the opposites-attract illusion, there are three possibilities. One is an eventual parting of the ways, all too often after many valuable years have been wasted. A second is the irrational non-action of staying together and being at each other's throats over an entire lifetime. The third is the worst possibility of all: compromise.

Compromising as a way of life (as opposed to occasionally giving in for rational, value-based reasons) usually results in both parties spending most of their time choosing between the lesser of two painful options. In reality, a compromise isn't really a compromise at all; it's a sacrifice. And, more often than not, a sacrifice isn't really a true sacrifice; it's an irrationally selfish act.

You and your mate should be spending the majority of your time doing things that bring both of you pleasure. If, instead, you are constantly at odds because your prime interests vary too widely, what better signal do you need to be convinced that you've made a mistake? The solution isn't to continue compromising, but to find someone whose interests are similar to yours. If you are already in an opposites-attract relationship that is causing you chronic pain instead of consistent pleasure, the only rational solution is to move on. Pay the price—in pain and discomfort—right now, and make it a clear and final payment.

THE HASSLE SIGNAL

With experience, you should become less and less willing to become involved in any situation that has the potential for the one activity you don't need in your life: hassling. If you're already in an unpleasant relationship, hassling is pretty hard to avoid, especially if your mate is hassle oriented.

A friend of mine is convinced that everyone has a Happiness Plug in the back of his head, and the reason some people can never seem to be happy is that their Plug has been pulled. The evidence, he insists, could clearly be observed in his ex-wife, who reveled in hassling, problem-finding, and general unhappiness. After many years of marriage, he became convinced that she had simply lost her Happiness Plug.

In a tongue-in-cheek manner, he said he believed there was an empty hole in her head which the plug had previously occupied, and that all her happiness fluid had been drained out. He claimed to have tried everything he could to make her happy, but to no avail. He half-jokingly said that if he had won a million dollars in the lottery, his ex-wife would have been depressed about having to pay taxes on it.

How can you tell if someone has lost his Happiness Plug? One way is to note how often you get boxed into can't-win situations with him. If your mate's Plug is missing, you're likely to continually find yourself facing the dilemma of "damned if you do and damned if you don't." If you are presently in such a relationship, you're in danger of becoming a victim of the I'm-Crazy, You're-Sane Theory. In a romantic relationship, not only are you a convenient target if your mate is neurotic, your ability to think rationally can be impaired by emotion.

I know whereof my friend speaks, because as a young man I endured the frustrating experience of dating a woman who clearly had her Happiness Plug pulled. People made her feel self-conscious, but a lack of people made her feel lonely; poverty depressed her, but having money made her feel guilty; she hated the routine of working, but not working made her feel inadequate. She was a great woman, except for one problem: Nothing could make her happy!

It was hassle, hassle, hassle—around the clock—day after day, week after week, month after month. I kept wanting to believe that modern medicine would come up with a technique for transplanting Happiness Plugs, but in the meantime my life was vanishing before my very eyes. One of our typical I'm-Crazy, You're-Sane conversations went something like this:

"Crazy" Tortoise: "Look at that rain. This is the worst storm I've seen in years."

"Sane" girlfriend: "It's not raining."

"Crazy" Tortoise: (Recovering quickly, as the rain begins to come down harder.) "Hmm . . . you're right. I guess I was mistaken. It's not raining."

"Sane" girlfriend: "I think you're trying to humor me. You know very well it's raining."

"Crazy" Tortoise: (Frantically thinking through all possibilities as he realizes he's getting trapped into another can't-win corner.) "You're right. It is raining. However, it's possible that the sun *may*

"Hmm, you're right. I guess I was mistaken. It's not raining."

eventually come out or—on the other hand—it *may* just continue to rain."

"Sane" girlfriend: "You think you're so clever by trying to humor me. Well, it won't work. Get stuffed!"

"Crazy" Tortoise: "Sorry."

Fortunately, I did not have access to a plastic bag and a rope. When your mate's Happiness Plug is missing, she will display a perverse delight in finding, if not artificially creating, can't-win situations for you. In the event you are presently in a can't-win relationship, the time to get out is *now*. Don't debate, don't argue, don't try to reason. The hassle-oriented person has the deck stacked against you before you even open your mouth, because she *wants* to be unhappy. Either understand that reality or be prepared to have your terrorist meter on red alert twenty-four hours a day.

THE LOOKING SIGNAL

By *looking*, I'm not just referring to an occasional stare at a beautiful woman or handsome man. I'm talking about looking for someone with whom you can become intimately involved. Some might argue that everyone is entitled to an occasional slip, but it's a dangerous precedent to set. If you're looking, the likelihood is that something isn't right.

What I find remarkable is the individual who regularly cheats on his spouse, yet claims to have a great marriage. It amazes me how many people delude themselves on this point. They will adamantly argue that infidelity has absolutely nothing whatsoever to do with their feelings toward their spouses.

I once had an acquaintance who put more effort into cheating on his wife than he put into his occupation. His office was in the city, his home in the suburbs—which was very convenient for him, since he had extracurricular activities lined up in the city four or five nights a week. Because his wife believed he had to work late most evenings, it was understandable to her that he was very tired on those rare nights when he was home.

Quite naturally, she assumed that his perpetual exhaustion was a result of putting in long, hard hours at the office (which, to some degree, was true, since many of his trysts did, in fact, take place right in his office).

He was an absolute genius at devising sophisticated schemes to assure that his affairs remained unknown to his wife. His most masterful ploy was the day he purposely rode to work with someone else and asked his wife to pick him up at the office at around 11:00 p.m. When she picked him up that night, he insisted on doing the driving. (Mind you, this was all premeditated, right down to the exhausted tone in his voice). As he drove home, he periodically pretended to doze off. Then, at just the right time, he deliberately ran off the road. (He had picked, days in advance, what he considered to be the perfect spot for a groggy swerve.) When his wife realized what was happening, she instinctively screamed and "awakened" him from his fake slumber.

In an Oscar-worthy performance, he feigned being startled, and it paid off handsomely. She immediately told him that it was far too dangerous for him to drive home late at night after putting in a grueling fifteen-hour day at the office, insisting that he stay in the city overnight whenever he had to work late (i.e., four or five nights a week). The clincher came the next day when she went out and bought him a suitcase to make sure he kept his promise to stay overnight when he was too tired to drive home. By the way— surprise!—they're no longer married. What's amazing is that his wife never did discover that he had cheated on her all those years.

Looking out for number one requires the ability to recognize and courage to acknowledge even the most painful and unpleasant realities. If you're looking, it's a warning sign that something is inherently wrong with your relationship. If so, it's critical to your happiness to summon the courage to analyze what the underlying problem is, then *do something about it.*

Whatever it is that caused your relationship to deteriorate probably took place over a long period of time, which is why it's usually very difficult, if not impossible, to correct the problem. More often than not, the rational solution, though most people dread facing up to it, is to terminate the relationship and look for a mate who satisfies your needs in a way that will eliminate the urge to look for greener pastures. I will never cease to be amazed at how many people stay in marriages that are clearly devoid of love.

THE RATIONALIZATION SIGNAL

Another acquaintance once told me that he had absolutely no affection for his wife. When I asked him the obvious—why he didn't get a divorce—he did not even make a pretense of trying to convince me that he had a good marriage. His sole reason for staying with her, he said, was that he loved his son too much to leave. I inquired as to how he could bear to face his wife every day under such awkward circumstances, to which he replied, "It's really not that bad. She doesn't get in my way. In fact, she hardly bothers me at all." Hmm . . . if the function of a husband or wife is to not get in the way, it's understandable why marriages are crashing on the rocks in record numbers.

THE EXIT

Hopefully, you're already convinced that carrying excess baggage can make your journey through life unnecessarily difficult, and an unhealthy love relationship constitutes very heavy baggage, indeed. It's spelled out simply in the **Crummy Love-Relationship Theory,** which is almost identical to the Crummy-Friendship Theory: *A crummy love relationship is one in which you consistently give more than you receive.*

If you are now in such relationship, do both your mate and your-self a favor by ending it before it does any more damage to either of you. Just because you've invested many years in a relationship that has caused you more pain than pleasure does not mean you should waste still more years of your life by continuing on. Don't be self-delusive by hiding from the truth in an effort to artificially smooth things over. Ignoring reality will only cause your relationship to get worse. You can't afford to leave the determination of your happiness in the hands of another person, especially your mate's. You, and you alone, should be in control of your destiny. If what I've said here applies to you, remember that the clock is ticking away the seconds of your life as you read these words.

There is virtually no excuse that justifies staying in an unhappy marriage or love relationship, and the worst excuse of all is children. If children are involved, you should remove yourself from your spouse's life so they can enjoy both of you at your best—in happier states than they now see you. If you stay together under miserable circumstances, not only will you and your spouse suffer, your children, who had nothing to do with the bad situation in which you now find yourselves, will be forced to endure the pain of watching the two of you constantly at odds. What they will be witnessing is a bad advertisement for marriage, which most certainly is not in their best interest.

We've already covered the phenomenon of guilt, so that shouldn't be a factor. You're both adults, and each of you had the right to say no to the relationship before the commitment became binding. The only justifiable reason for feeling guilty is if you irrationally try to hold together the pieces of a crumbling relationship, thus unnecessarily causing more discomfort to your mate. You have no right to make your partner suffer any longer, even if he or she erroneously believes that it's best to stay together. Usually such a thought on the part of your mate is caused by irrational self-interest, which in turn is caused by the emotion of fear. Change can be a scary thing, and it grows ever scarier as you become more and more accustomed to a set way of life.

What a person is today, and what you feel for her today, are realities—and that cuts both ways. If, for example, you were an honest, faithful husband for ten years, it might be reasonable to expect your wife to forgive you for being unfaithful once. But if it becomes an addiction at age forty, a rational woman realizes that what you did yesterday was what you were *yesterday*. What you do today is what you are *today*. If your wife had rational reasons for loving you yesterday, those reasons are no longer valid if you are not the same individual you were in the past. Sure, you accumulate a certain number of credits over the years for good deeds, but never do you build up a big enough backlog to give you the right to continually mistreat your spouse.

People change with time. When two individuals grow in different directions, they end up looking at strangers across the dinner table. Their divergent growths normally take place over a period of many years, making it unnoticeable on a day-to-day basis. As a result, it's impractical—if not impossible—to retrace your steps and teach one another everything you've learned over a long period of time. You may have started out as two individuals with similar interests, but evolved into a classic opposites-attract couple.

There's only one relevant factor to consider when determining whether you're in a crummy love relationship: Does your Weight-and-Balance Happiness Scale tell you that what you are getting out of the relationship is worth what you are putting into it? No matter how good the good is, if the bad outweighs it, you're in a crummy love relationship. And staying in a crummy love relationship can be a fatal blow to your efforts to look out for number one.

The responsible thing to do is to take action to terminate a bad relationship *before* you find a better one. By doing so, you not only increase your chances of finding the right person, you ease the pain for everyone involved. The all-too-frequent mistake of waiting until the kids are grown (and the woman is past her prime) is the most irrationally selfish action a husband can take. Such a man not only wastes the best years of his own life, but also cheats his spouse of her youth and subjects innocent children to a daily lie. With such a scenario playing out so regularly, is it any wonder why so many children grow up with serious emotional issues?

Once you sever a bad relationship, it frees both you and your mate to search for a better life, so it's a win-win situation.

LOOKING BACK

If you've decided your love relationship is fundamentally unsound and have made a rational decision to terminate it, allow me to offer one piece of advice with regard to looking back: Don't! There's almost always a temptation to go back and give it one more try. I suppose anything is possible, but the reality is that it seldom works out.

One of the biggest influences that can cause a person to rationalize a bad relationship is thinking about all the pain involved in searching for another mate. To someone who has been away from the search-and-rejection game for many years, the prospect of having to go through it all over again can be disconcerting to an extreme. There's only one thing I can think of that's worse: a continued lifetime of dull, nagging nothingness. Better to be alive and hurting than to endure a living death day in and day out.

THE SEARCH

First and foremost, never allow a failed romance to cloud your thinking. Your life is too important to be destroyed by circumstances beyond your control, especially if those circumstances have to do with the quirks of another human being. Once you've put your old romance behind you, the chances of finding the right person improve in direct proportion to the amount of time, effort, and patience you invest. The overriding question becomes: Am I willing—at age thirty . . . or forty . . . or older—to pay the price for a better life? In the end, it always gets down to price-paying.

As with friends, if you haven't been able to find love, the likelihood is that you haven't tried hard enough. There are plenty of roses among the weeds out there, but they will never discover you without your exerting a great deal of effort. It's up to you to take matters into your own hands and do the discovering. Whether you've never been in love or are now in a bad relationship and longing to discover true love, the one thing you can be certain of is that it's out there.

Of course, you can't expect to find the right person if you don't know what you're looking for. And to know that, you first have to know yourself. You must be totally honest with yourself about who you are and what you want out of life. This self-examination should be done when your intellect is in control. If you allow emotions to guide your thoughts, you're likely to delude yourself. Self-examination, when undertaken in a heightened emotional state, can produce dangerous illusions. You must be prepared to stare reality in the face. Once you do that, it becomes a matter of exercising the self-discipline to stick to your rational conclusions when your emotions start hammering away at your otherwise sound judgment.

LONELINESS

The most dangerous emotion in this regard is the empty feeling of loneliness. Loneliness for love is a potential panic situation, and panic is an emotional state you should avoid at all costs if your objective is to find true love. Loneliness for love is an empty feeling that is impossible to adequately describe with mere words, yet just about everyone has experienced it. As with friendship, you won't be able to fully enjoy a love relationship if you equate aloneness with loneliness.

If you allow your loneliness for love to get out of control, you become vulnerable to the possibility of convincing yourself that you're in love with someone with whom you really aren't. It's been said that millions of people spend their lives in misery out of the fear of dying alone. They may not think about it consciously, or even admit it to themselves, but the price they pay for not being alone at the time of death is a lifetime of joyless coexistence.

Some people try to cope with the panic of loneliness by taking the volume approach to finding love. But, in truth, this strategy is as far removed from real love as one can get. Spreading yourself too thin only succeeds in creating the kind of lonely feeling one often experiences at a large social gathering. Some of the loneliest-looking people I've ever seen have been so-called ladies' men. The chances of finding the kind of love gratification you seek are much better if you have the self-discipline and patience to concentrate on finding one great human being to whom you are genuinely attracted rather than trying to suppress your loneliness with high volume.

LAW OF AVERAGES

Just as you don't need any specific client, customer, or job, neither do you need any specific individual as a lifetime partner. While it's true that you only need to find one person, that doesn't mean there is only one person available. If you insist on believing there is only one man or woman in the whole world who is right for you, you put yourself under an enormous amount of unnecessary pressure.

It's no different than when you fall into the business trap of believing that the deal you're working on is the only deal in the world. Once you convince yourself of that, there's a tendency to press. And the harder one presses, the worse his chances of success. If a love relationship doesn't work out, the reality is that there *is* another one just around the next corner. The rational thing to do is to forget about the one that got away and get on with your search for someone else.

There will be times when the odds against finding that one special person seem so overwhelming that it's hard to keep the faith, but always remember that it's a very big world out there. Keep reminding yourself that you only need to find one right person, and, in that regard, the law of averages is on your side.

No two people are exactly alike, so you're absolutely right if you think you will never find another love like the one you had. You won't, but what you will find is a different love, one that can bring you happiness in many new ways. Which is why you should not make the mistake of trying to compare a new love with an old one. It's the apples-and-oranges fallacy again. The truth of the matter is that there are many people with whom you can fall genuinely in love.

EFFORT

If you're serious about finding love, the first thing you should do is turn off the television set, get up out of your chair, and explore what's out there. Life isn't long enough for you to sit around and mope about how lonely you are. The time to start searching is now.

Try new places ... new experiences ... new people. If you haven't previously put forth any meaningful effort in this area, you'll be amazed at the variety of activities that await you, activities you may not have known about or things you never seriously considered doing before. There's a lot more to life than eating, sleeping, working, going out to dinner once a week, and taking in an occasional movie. It's critical that you be willing to try new experiences.

Anyone who has ever gone fishing knows all too well what a tricky proposition it is. You have to use the right pole, the proper bait, and cast your line just right. To talk about it is easy; to actually do it can be very difficult. Likewise, that's part of the price you must pay for finding the right person with whom to share your life. If you are not willing to pay the price, be forewarned that there are millions of competitors who are. Those who are willing to make the greatest investment of time, energy, rejection, and embarrassment in the Free-Enterprise Love Market are the ones who will reap the greatest rewards. Those who are not willing to make such an investment should be prepared to live without love or, worse, to live with someone under a false pretense of love.

REJECTION

One of the greatest barriers that prevents males and females from getting together is the fear of rejection. If only we could find a way to insulate our delicate egos from coming apart at the seams when faced with something as ghoulish as rejection. What's silly about it is that in most cases the other person isn't even rejecting you; she's rejecting a stranger.

Prerelationship fears of rejection can close the door on a new experience before it's even begun. One especially self-protective device is the standoffish approach to a first meeting, even to the extreme of refusing to show an interest in someone you've just met out of the fear that your interest may not be reciprocated. At a minimum, this is a self-defeating fear. People can't read your mind, so if you fail to display an interest, it will be assumed you have none.

Prerelationship fears are often a result of a post-relationship feeling of rejection. Once you've been burned, it's hard to subject yourself to the possibility of being hurt again. If you are not able to deal with lost love, the intensity of this fear is likely to increase with each love relationship that goes sour. Unfortunately, many people become hardened with age, which results in their being more defensive, more cautious, less open, less relaxed, and less themselves when meeting members of the opposite sex. Pain is not something that human beings instinctively try to avoid.

Nevertheless, though it's a paradox of sorts, part of the price of finding pleasure and avoiding pain is to be willing to undertake the risk of rejection. It's not a very appealing thought, but, unfortunately, it's part of life. Because love is one of the greatest joys human beings can experience, it quite naturally carries with it a big price tag. It seems almost sadistic that nature asks us to go through so much rejection, pain, and effort without guaranteeing us we will succeed in finding, let alone keeping, the love we seek.

TRUTH IN ADVERTISING

Even if you are willing to make the effort and are able to keep rejection in perspective, the other person still has to recognize you when you come into view. Be careful not to get so caught up in trying new activities that you forget there are members of the opposite sex who will like you for exactly who and what you are. Don't fake a lifestyle just because it seems to work for someone else. You are *not* someone else, and to misrepresent yourself is a big mistake. A relationship that evolves from an initial attraction based on misrepresentation will explode in your face when the real you is discovered—which is guaranteed to happen, sooner rather than later.

The nice thing about advertising your true self is that you may be able to compensate for the other party in the event she makes the mistake of trying to put on a false front. Suppose you're a man who likes the quiet type and enjoys intellectual stimulation and good one-on-one conversation. You have somehow ended up at a wild party where just about everyone there is acting like a high school kid at his first social gathering, but there happens to be a woman at the party who is quiet, intellectual, and enjoys good one-on-one conversation.

The only problem is that you don't know she's there, because even though she doesn't enjoy the fast-lane lifestyle, she's acting out the role of swinger in the mistaken belief that it's in her best interest to conform to her surroundings. But because *you* understand why it's so important to advertise your real self, you are easily recognizable to everyone present. As a result, the intellectual-in-swinger's-disguise may just find *you* even if you aren't able to find *her*.

The perfect location for the false-advertising game is the so-called singles bar, which is an indoor version of the Thousanduplets phenomenon I experienced in Manhattan Beach when I was single. When it comes to finding serious love, you could not ask for a worse atmosphere than a singles bar. The main problem is that most everyone there is working feverishly in an attempt to imitate everyone else. Some might argue that the odds are good in a singles bar because of the sheer volume, which is probably true if one's objective is to see how many members of the opposite sex he can seduce. However, if your objective is to find lasting love, the law of averages are overwhelmingly against you in such a plastic environment.

OBSTACLES

Old Man Murphy's ghost is fond of placing obstacles in strategic spots leading up to the Love Hurdle, hoping he can distract his prey just long enough to cause him to trip over it. Following are some of the more common—and dangerous—of Murphy's obstacles to avoid when trying to clear the Love Hurdle.

THE WHAT-OTHERS-THINK OBSTACLE

With all the inherent problems associated with clearing the Love Hurdle, the last thing in the world you need are the opinions of others. It's perfectly natural to feel good when others think highly of your mate, but if such opinions are of primary importance to you, you're caught in the intimidation-through-conformity trap.

In the event you decide to solicit the advice of friends regarding matters of love, you had better be very certain about who your real friends are. Never forget the reality that misery loves company. Many insecure, unhappy people find comfort in knowing that others are unhappy, too. The question you must ask yourself is: If a friend advises me to give up someone I love, can he or she furnish me with a satisfactory replacement? Since you are the one who will have to endure the pain of a wrong decision, best you make your own decision and take third-party opinions with a grain of salt—if at all.

I recall having a friend in college who managed to win over the most sought-after co-ed on campus. She was absolutely perfect— just what every *other* guy at the school wanted. After the wedding, my friend put his trophy on the mantel and waited for . . . well, I guess he wasn't exactly sure what he was waiting for. What he got, however, was just about everything he never wanted. He finally concluded that what he had won was what *others* wanted, which had nothing whatsoever to do with what *he* wanted.

Men and women are not trophies to be won. They are people— individuals who have unique needs and who represent potential values to you to the extent they can fill *your* needs. Trying to win the affection of a woman just because every other guy seems to desire her is an irrational objective that can reap a lifetime of unanticipated pain.

The corollary to the trophy syndrome is the mistake of pursuing a woman just because you find her physically attractive. Good looks have a way of fading as age overtakes us, and when the glow disappears, all that's left is a human being. Unfortunately, many people wait far too long before finally admitting to themselves that their spouse is not the person with whom they want to spend the rest of their life.

THE BOY-GIRL OBSTACLE

The Boy-Girl Obstacle applies to all facets of life, but derives its name from the fact that its workings are most visible in matters of love. Its roots lie in the **Boy-Girl Theory,** which states: *Everyone wants what he can't have and does not want what he can have.* It's a dangerous human trait made possible by man's unique ability to delude himself. Unfortunately, it can have devastating effects on an individual's life. The Boy-Girl Obstacle has a tendency to repress the rational parts of our minds and replace them with irrational desires to seek forbidden fruit.

It could just as easily be called the Sucker Syndrome, because a sucker is precisely what one feels like when he comes out of the ether and realizes that he's been steered off his rational course by emotion. You've stumbled over the Boy-Girl Obstacle when your mind plays tricks on you by making you believe you're in love with someone just because she plays "hard to get." The same is true when you push someone out of your life just because she's readily available to you, even though she may possess many qualities you greatly admire.

It's virtually impossible to totally repress the Boy-Girl instinct, but, with a bit of effort, one can develop the self-discipline to at least keep it under control. It also takes a rational mind to be able to honestly analyze whether you desire someone because she's playing hard to get or because she possesses values that you genuinely admire and respect. The sad reality is that the Boy-Girl Obstacle is a condition rampant among otherwise mature adults, which makes their trip over the Love Hurdle extremely difficult.

Then there's the other side of the coin—the individual who takes the easy way out and marries someone out of habit, the habit of having been with her over a long period of time. In such a case, love is not the issue so much as convenience. It's easy for two people to become so accustomed to one another that homeostasis (the tendency to live with existing conditions and avoid change) sets in. The mere thought of having to go out into the harsh world and start searching all over again is a major incentive for someone to take the easy way out and opt to stay where he is.

The chronic nothingness that often results from such an arrangement is a sad way to live one's life. Regardless of how long you've been with someone, the only valid reason for staying together is love. If you don't feel the excitement that is an essential ingredient of the emotion of love, you should be questioning whether you're really in love with the other person. Unless your reason for staying with someone is that you admire and respect her, and that she satisfies your highest values and needs, you're in the wrong place.

Love is not a subject you can afford to address in a cavalier manner, so be careful not to allow your emotions to delude you. Extreme cases of the Boy-Girl Obstacle are most prevalent in people who have a low reading on their awareness meters.

THE INFATUATION OBSTACLE

Emotions have a way of clouding reality and repressing logic. You have to learn to deal with your emotions head-on, through rational thought, in order to control them. If you allow your emotions to guide your actions too often, the results can be catastrophic. This is especially true in matters of love. When you become physically attracted to someone without giving much thought as to whether she represents values you hold in high esteem, it means that your intellect is on sick leave.

Physical attraction is the phenomenon that most often produces the illusion of love. Unfortunately, it usually takes a long time to realize that it's sex alone that attracts you to another person and that there is no real love involved. Beware: All too often, two martinis can cause one to confuse sexual attraction with love. What I'm talking about here is a phenomenon commonly referred to as *infatuation*—an illusion that occurs most frequently between the ages of thirteen and thirty. Unfortunately, many people carry infatuation symptoms well into their fifties or sixties, which can be both embarrassing and costly. Infatuation does not wear well on grandfatherly types.

Infatuation can be a threat to one's health, financial well-being, and happiness. My most memorable experience with this menacing health hazard occurred in an earlier life when I was a young, single, impetuous tortoise. It was at a time when I was roaming the streets of New York, searching for wealthy investors who might be willing to listen to my hallucinations about big-money deals. I occasionally found time for a little entertainment, and at my tender age I was still able to burn the candle at both ends.

One day, my ever-watchful eye brought me in contact with a stunningly beautiful young lady of Puerto Rican descent who had *infatuation* stamped across her forehead. Unfortunately, it was written in Spanish, a language I didn't speak. Ignorantly, I just assumed that the word was *love*. I had recently seen the stage version of *West Side Story*, so I was ripe for the Infatuation Trap, particularly one in which the Broadway musical came to life before my very eyes. I was the reptilian equivalent of Clark Kent, periodically entering a phone booth and emerging as Supertortoise. I would visit Harold Hart during the day, talk about big business deals, then emerge from his Park Avenue apartment as Tony, straight out of *West Side Story*. As you can imagine, transforming the target of my infatuation into Maria was a rather easy task.

When your emotions are in control, you're in danger of doing things you wouldn't even consider doing under normal circumstances. In my case, after several romantic lunches at the local automat, I managed one evening to end up on the fourth floor of an old tenement house on the Lower East Side of Manhattan—a building with no fire escape and no elevator. There I was, in a dark, tiny apartment with only one exit. I tell you, tortoises were never meant to be in situations like that.

Then it came—the knock at the door at 4:00 a.m., a knock that soon turned into a ferocious banging interspersed with Spanish words I couldn't understand. There was, however, no doubt in my mind that the person at the door was not serenading us with "Spanish Eyes." In a voice that would not cause anyone to mistake me for Rambo, I asked Maria, "Wh . . . Who is th . . . that?" In a cavalier tone, she answered, "My husband." No problem, I thought to myself. I'll just hold my breath until I become asphyxiated. That way, I'll never have to know what I looked like when the man on the other side of the door got through rearranging my body parts.

I frantically searched for clothes in the dark—mine, hers, his—any clothes! After partially covering my body with a variety of garments that made me look like a candidate for first prize at the annual Lower East Side Halloween Costume Contest, Maria opened the door and—yikes!—let him in. The moment of truth was upon me. What should I do? Tortoises aren't fast; I had no weapons; and I'm hardly a master at fisticuffs, particularly on the fourth floor of a tenement house at four o'clock in the morning. And who would I be facing—the reincarnation of Zorro?

While Maria began explaining to her husband that I was a priest from Jersey City, I gave a sort of half-salute greeting as I casually edged my way toward the door. As their conversation heated up, I kept right on edging . . . and edging . . . and edging. When it was all over, I had set two track-and-field records that still stand today. One was the time for a reptile descending four flights of tenement-house stairs—3.5 seconds. The other was the time elapsed covering the distance between Avenue B and First Avenue in the snow—conditions: after midnight, with no wind at the runner's back—twenty seconds. And, mind you, all this was accomplished while wearing only one shoe!

Finally, a bit of good luck—a taxi zipped by at that ominous hour. I flagged it down, jumped in, and yelled, "Hit it!" As the taxi sped out of sight toward mid-town civilization, the saga of Tony the Tortoise faded into the night, never to be heard from again.

Moral: Beware of infatuation. It can lead to dangers you haven't even dreamed of, but which can permanently impair your capacity to look out for number one.

THE "FALLING IN LOVE WITH LOVE" OBSTACLE

Even when love is real, it has an illusory quality about it. The reason love mirages abound is because our thirst for love is so insatiable. This often leads to the phenomenon of "falling in love with love."

If you find yourself falling in love every time you have too much to drink, the chances are excellent that you're in the habit of falling in love with love. Unfortunately, love is an abstract, so it

"Fernando, I'd like you to meet Father Torteesia from Jersey City."

doesn't make a very good partner. It can't go to a movie with you; it can't converse with you; it can't have a good laugh with you. Nevertheless, so long as you have a pulse rate, love will always be a bit illusory. Realizing that, it's wise to be vigilant about not becoming so addicted to the emotion of love that you imagine it's the real thing every time a pretty face crosses your path.

THE TRANSFORMATION OBSTACLE

Nothing is more frustrating than being in love with—or, worse, thinking you're in love with—someone who isn't precisely what you would like her to be. The failure to accept the reality of who and what your mate really is can lead to one of two irrational acts on your part, and both of them are dangerous.

The first is to try to imagine your mate being something other than what she really is. The second is to try to *mold* her into being what you want her to be. In either case, the problem is that you violate the laws of nature. The first is a matter of deluding yourself, the second an attempt to tamper with the impossible. Worse, the latter is based on the rather arrogant assumption that you possess the right to change someone based on your subjective standards. You don't.

A friend of mine once dated a woman whom he rated a ten in eight categories on his ten-highest-values list. Unfortunately, she rated no better than a one in the other two categories. Because of her high ratings in eight areas, he was highly motivated to ignore her two failing marks. That would have been bad enough, but when he made the mistake of attempting to help her correct (to his satisfaction) her two "problem" areas, the result was predictable. When you start "helping" a person to change, it tends to escalate a mildly unhappy relationship into an emotional holocaust.

The point is that irrespective of the number of admirable qualities a person may possess, it does not make her not-so-admirable qualities disappear. And it certainly doesn't mean you can change those qualities—or that you have the right to. Best you forget about altering your mate's undesirable traits. Anything is possible, but assuming she is not going to change is as close as you can get to a sure thing. The rational way to look at the matter is to weigh your mate's existing pluses and minuses against each other, then allow your Weight-and-Balance Happiness Scale to provide you with the verdict.

LOVE HOMICIDE

Sadly, many people are fortunate enough to find love, only to turn around and destroy it. This sad situation often comes about through jealousy, possessiveness, or interfering with the growth of a mate, to name but a few of the better-known causes.

If you've had a tough time trying to get over the Love Hurdle, the first place to look, as always, is in the mirror. Are you sure your lack of success isn't a result of your not being willing to make the effort to get out and look, to endure the pain that comes with rejection, or to contribute significant value to a prospective partner's Weight-and-Balance Happiness Scale? You should be brutally honest with yourself when conducting this self-examination, because your long-term happiness is at stake. Love is not a favor to be automatically bestowed upon you by the party of your choice. If your life has been thin on love, there's a good chance you haven't worked hard enough to earn it.

You should also keep in mind that it's difficult to earn love from someone until you've earned it from yourself. A meaningful love relationship requires self-esteem. Authentic love is an expression of one's admiration of qualities exhibited by another individual, qualities that more often than not are reflective of one's own most admirable traits.

And a trait that is of special importance is self-respect. Again, you develop self-respect by consciously thinking through your values, then having the self-discipline to stick by them—regard-less of the circumstances. When you refuse to compromise your integrity, the other person is likely to view your self-discipline with admiration and respect.

Also, never lose sight of the fact that you and your mate are not a single entity. You cannot always think alike, agree on every issue, or have interests that coincide 100 percent of the time. In fact, if it were possible for you to be completely in harmony with your mate, you would likely have a dull, unhealthy relationship. People who strive for such oneness reflect a basic insecurity in themselves and invite problems into their lives. David Seabury put it well when he explained:

> Love is not so simple and malleable as many suppose. Put it in prison and it dies. Restrict it and it turns into hate. Force it and it disappears. You cannot will love, nor even control it. You can only guide its expression. It comes or it goes according to those qualities in life that invite it or deny its presence.

EARNING YOUR WAY

As you would expect, the building blocks of a sound love relationship are pretty much the same as those of a sound friendship: admiration, respect, and rational self-interest. I don't think it's possible to have a healthy love relationship with someone you do not admire and respect.

When it comes to love, self-discipline, patience, and rational self-interest have the potential to yield a bigger payoff than in any other area of your life. As would be expected, the price/reward ratio asserts itself here, so it's important not to become lax and take love for granted once you've found it. Simply going through the motions doesn't work. Nurturing a worthwhile love relationship takes *conscious* effort.

9 The Starting Line

Now that I think about it, I'm glad life is not as Madison Avenue portrays it, because writing this book has reminded me just how exciting and wonderful real life can be. And that, above all else, is what I hope you have gotten from these pages—that by clearing life's major hurdles, you can achieve a truly joyful existence in which the pleasures you experience far exceed the pain you occasionally endure. What greater epitaph than to be able to say that when you passed this way, you enjoyed life to the fullest extent possible without harming anyone else?

By now I think you know that all this will not happen by accident. To clear life's hurdles requires a great deal of effort. Effort is the price, happiness the reward. It takes effort to be aware; it takes effort to make conscious, rational decisions; it takes effort not to delude yourself by feeding incorrect information to your Weight-and-Balance Happiness Scale; it takes effort to concentrate on the *is's* of life and ignore the *ought to's* that continually tempt you to stray from a rational course.

In addition to effort, it takes courage—the courage to change an established way of life and move on to a better one. You begin to summon that courage when you place your problems in proper perspective. Few problems are insurmountable. There is almost always a way out—a way of getting from where you are now to where you want to be in life. It's not impossible to make changes, just hard. Compromising will not do it; sweeping irritations under the rug will not do it; continuing to load yourself down with excess baggage will not do it.

What *will* do it is price paying. You must be willing to make a serious commitment to do whatever it takes to set your life on a winning course. You must be willing to pay the price of trying unique experiences, some of which will cause you pain. Others, however, will lead to pleasures beyond anything you may have imagined. Pay the price of looking around the People Store, and connect with as many roses as possible. They will add untold happiness to your life if you are willing to deal with others on a mutually beneficial basis.

As to the weeds in your life, best you leave them in the People Store for someone else to invite into his life. Those who would harass you, annoy you, or intimidate you—through credentials, custom and tradition, conformity, guilt, or any other ploy—have no place in your plans to look out for number one. Unfortunately, problem people will sometimes invite themselves into your life without your approval. But always keep in mind that they can only bother until you make the decision not to allow them to.

Above all, when you believe you are finally ready to start clearing life's hurdles, don't allow anyone to hold you back. And once you get down in the starting blocks, no short-term patching allowed. When I say *starting blocks*, I'm talking about the starting blocks on a track that leads to long-term solutions. When you spring forward toward that first hurdle, make self-discipline and patience your trademarks. Be willing to pay the full price for love, friendship, and financial gain so your life will not be a perpetual rerun at the hurdles that now stand between your present circumstances and where you want to be.

Oops . . . I almost forgot Old Man Murphy. Always remember that he's out there . . . lurking in the shadows . . . plotting to trip you up. At heart, Murphy is really just a playful old trickster. I sometimes suspect that he secretly enjoys seeing people thwart his little pranks. I believe he actually admires those who take his best shots, then pick themselves up, brush themselves off, and continue to move forward more determined than ever. Rest assured that Murphy and nature will continue to see to it that circumstances change, but once you get the hang of it, you'll be able to handle the phenomenon of change as though it was an everyday occurrence—which it is.

All right, enough talk. It's time to get down in the starting blocks. And when you do, keep in mind that the clock does not begin ticking when you lunge forward. It's *already* ticking! If you have the ability to make conscious, rational decisions, the only question that remains is: Do you have the *courage*?

You have every right to enjoy a lifetime of happiness, so be good to yourself and enjoy each moment to the fullest. Tomorrow will come soon enough and bring with it its share of sorrows. The past no longer exists; the future is a question mark; the only reality is the present.

Personally, I believe you are deserving of the joy that comes from looking out for number one. How can I make such a statement if I don't even know you? Because I believe that every individual has the right to seek happiness so long as he does not forcibly interfere in the lives of others. So begin today to do good deeds for that person in the mirror whom you have probably neglected far too long. To paraphrase a well-known, pop-psyche television personality, *self really does matter.* The world may not owe you a living, but you owe yourself the world.

Good luck . . . and watch out for your toes as you go over each hurdle. If you happen to trip over one of them, not to worry. Simply pick yourself up and keep trying until you clear it, because Old Man Murphy is just testing you. If you refuse to give up, it's just a matter of time until he begins to respect you and allows you to move on. And when you've cleared all the hurdles and broken the tape, it's not the finish line you will have reached; it's the *starting line*—the beginning of a life where rational dreams have a way of coming true.

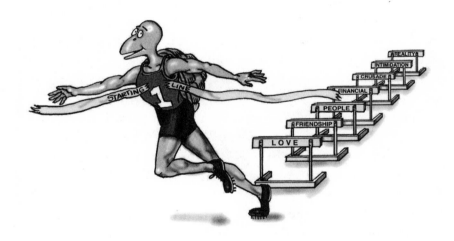

Robert Ringer is an American icon whose insights into life have helped more people transform their aspirations and goals into reality than perhaps any other author in history. For more than three decades, his works have stood alone as the gospel when it comes to conveying worldly wisdom to millions of readers worldwide.

He is the author of two *New York Times* #1 bestsellers, both of which have been listed by *The New York Times* among the 15 best-selling motivational books of all time. He is also the publisher of RobertRinger.com, where he combines philosophy, reality, and action in his trademark style that translates into tangible results for his readers.

Ringer has appeared on numerous national television and radio shows, including *The Tonight Show, Today, The Dennis Miller Show, Good Morning America, ABC Nightline,* and *The Charlie Rose Show,* and has made a variety of appearances on Fox News and Fox Business.

He has also been the subject of feature articles in such major publications as *Time, People, The Wall Street Journal, Fortune, Barron's,* and *The New York Times.*

To learn about Robert Ringer's life-changing new program, Fast Track to Dealmaking Fortunes, visit www.robertringer.com/products/fast-track-to-dealmaking-fortunes.